DEDICATION
This book is lovingly dedicated to GNBA Ministry Partners. You help us through your prayers and financial support to take the message of Christ to places where radio does it best.

RESOURCES
Receive a Free Copy of Sounding Out
A free bi-monthly newsletter mailed by GNBA. It keeps you up-to-date with current programmes and reports on the outcome of the ministry. Devotional articles are also included.
Receive Free Transcripts
Many radio programmes are available as free transcripts to an email address. Twice a month sermons (usually by Derek Stringer) are made available as devotional resources. Give us your email address and you can join the worldwide family of believers taking these transcripts.
Receive a Bi-Monthly CD
By becoming a Ministry Partner with GNBA you will receive a bi-monthly CD packed with helpful Bible resources, including a message from Derek Stringer.

Printed and bound in Great Britain by
www.berforts.com
Stevenage

Good News Broadcasting Association (GB)
Ranskill DN22 8NN England
Telephone: (0) 1777817138
Email: info@gnba.net Internet: www.gnba.net

Discovering Great Secrets

Discovering Great Secrets

PREFACE

Alasdaire MacIntyre compares the situation that the church is in to that of a person standing at a bus stop who is approached by a complete stranger who says, *"The Latin name of the common wild duck is histrionicus, histrionicus, histrionicus."* The meaning of the sentence is clear enough, but without a larger context, *"a broader framework of meaning,"* it just doesn't make much sense. It would make sense if the stranger had confused the person he was talking to with another person he had met at the bus stop before who in the course of their prior conversation had asked, *"Say, by any chance would you happen to know the Latin name of the common duck?"* And it would make sense if the stranger who spoke to the other person at the bus stop was in therapy dealing with his problem with shyness and had been told to try to strike up conversations with people he didn't know by saying the first thing that came to mind. And it would make sense if the stranger was a spy who had made arrangements to meet a contact at that bus stop and his code was the Latin name of the common wild duck. But without knowing the back story, the statement, while sensible enough, remains meaningless.

So, what's the story of our faith? What helps us put the puzzle together? Read on and perhaps it will be a secret no more.

Discovering Great Secrets

Chapter 1
DISCOVER THE GREAT SECRET
Start-Up Steps To Living A Christian Life

Most people love a good mystery, that's why Agatha Christie has such a long-running play in the West End of London and years after her death, her books and TV dramas go down well. As well as doing things like crosswords and Sudoku many people enjoy trying to solve mysteries or puzzles. Let me give you an example of one and see if you can solve it before you read on.

A carrot, a football scarf and five buttons were found in a field. If nobody placed them there, how did they arrive?
Do you know the answer? Well, the solution to the mystery is:
They were the remains of a snowman after the thaw.

I heard a funny story about a man who attended the first night of a theatrical performance of a new mystery. Unfortunately, he was seated on the back row in a poor seat. He called an usher over and said, "I LOVE to figure out mysteries, so if there is any way you could move me to a seat down front, I'll give you a handsome tip." The usher saw money signs and happened to know that one of the regular patrons wasn't using his seat that night. He said, "Right this way, sir!" After he was escorted by the usher to a seat in the middle of the third row, the mystery-lover handed the usher a 20 pence coin and said, "Thanks." The usher frowned at the 20 pence and then said to him as he walked away, "By the way, the butler did it!"

For many mysteries, finding the answer takes away the interest or importance of the whole thing but that's certainly not true of the mystery that I'm talking about!

The word 'mystery' appears 27 times in the New Testament but in the Bible, 'mystery' doesn't mean something that is always hidden. It describes a truth that was secret once, but at the proper time it is disclosed. And don't worry, we are going to

Discovering Great Secrets

discover the secret to this mystery but I want to start by giving you a few clues to see if you can discover it for yourself.

CLUE 1: ONCE DOWN IT HELPS ME UP

The secret behind this mystery is so amazing it can make us smile in the most difficult times of our life.

The apostle Paul tells us in 2 Corinthians, he had been beaten eight times, shipwrecked three times, and once was stoned so badly people thought that he was dead. Did he grumble about his suffering? No - he discovered joy in his suffering! He had found a mystery that helped him handle pain and trials with a positive attitude. Paul wrote, "I rejoice in what was suffered for you" (Colossians 1:24). He wanted to be free to preach and start churches, but he had found a secret that helped him to see a different perspective. While sitting in prison chained to a soldier, waiting to be executed, he wrote letters to Philemon, his friend and helper, and to the Christians at Ephesus, Philippi and Colossae.

Have we discovered the secret? Have you uncovered the mysterious power that enables you not to just survive the tough times of life, but to thrive during them?

CLUE 2: ONCE HIDDEN IT'S NOW REVEALED

This mystery is not something that has always been known. Paul writes, "The mystery that has been hidden for ages and generations, but is now disclosed." This mystery wasn't understood by people in Old Testament times. The Old Testament is full of promises from God that He will save and deliver His people. What you never find in the Old Testament is HOW God intended to do it. That part was hidden – it was a mystery. For example, I love the promise of God given in Isaiah 40 where He says, "Those who hope in the Lord will renew their strength. They will soar on wings like eagles; they will run and not grow weary, they will walk and not be faint." That's an absolute promise of God, but HOW does He actually strengthen

Discovering Great Secrets

His children? Isaiah couldn't answer that question; it was a mystery.

David communicated the wonderful promise in the 23rd Psalm that "goodness and mercy shall follow me all the days of my life." That's true, of course, but he would have been stumped if you had asked him, "Okay, I believe the promise but, O King, please tell me how does God do that?" David might have stabbed at an answer – but he really couldn't give the correct answer, because during his time it was still a mystery, hidden for the ages. But now I know how God does it, and you can too, when you learn the mystery. Any guesses yet?

CLUE 3: ONCE LACKING I'M NOW COMPLETE

Paul describes the reason for which this mystery is revealed – "so that we may present everyone perfect in Christ." The word *perfect* doesn't mean without flaw. Paul uses it to mean "whole." In Old Testament times people lived under the law. The only way to try to be a complete person was to keep the law. They existed with an achievement mentality in which righteousness was linked to how good or bad they were. But this mystery offers a new understanding.

There are churches that communicate a performance standard. They have simply re-introduced the Old Testament law. They still state that salvation is a matter of "thou shalt" and "thou shalt not." People trying to live under this old performance standard punish themselves in the process. Their motto is: TRY HARDER! This is a formula for failure. In a soccer game a player missed an easy but important shot. He became so angry he punched himself on the chin. I know the feeling, as does anyone who has played sport. I could almost hear the player saying, "You idiot! Try harder!" He really is the picture of everyone who thinks salvation is about performance. This mystery completely cancels out the performance standard principle. This mystery is the only way we can ever become a complete person.

Discovering Great Secrets

Have you discovered the secret yet? If you haven't, it's in Paul's letter to the Colossians. All three clues are contained in this passage (Colossians 1:24 to 29).

"Now I rejoice in what was suffered for you, and I fill up in my flesh what is still lacking in regard to Christ's afflictions, for the sake of his body, which is the church. I have become its servant by the commission God gave me to present to you the word of God in its fullness - the MYSTERY that has been kept hidden for ages and generations, but is now disclosed to the saints. To them God has chosen to make known among the Gentiles the glorious riches of this mystery, which is CHRIST IN YOU, the hope of glory. We proclaim him, admonishing and teaching everyone with all wisdom, so that we may present everyone perfect in Christ. To this end I labour, struggling with all his energy, which so powerfully works in me."

This is the great secret - CHRIST IN YOU.

I first discovered the power of this profound mystery from reading books like *The Saving Life of Christ* by Major Ian Thomas. The New Testament teaches the dual truths of how we are "in Christ" and how Christ is also "in us." Major Thomas expressed it this way:
"To be in Christ– that makes you fit for heaven; but for Christ to be in you – that makes you fit for earth!
To be in Christ–that changes your destination; but for Christ to be in you – that changes your destiny!
To be in Christ makes heaven your home; but for Christ to be in you makes this world God's workshop."

That's the great secret! Once grasped it changes the way we understand the Christian life. I want to consider three enormous personal applications.

FIRST: THERE IS PRESERVATION

Salvation is Jesus living in us! Jesus stunned the religious leaders by saying, "The Kingdom of God is within you." He

Discovering Great Secrets

wasn't talking about some kind of divine spark. He was talking about a preservation order stamped on our lives when the Lord and Saviour comes to live inside us.

Robert Boyd Munger wrote a little booklet entitled, *"My Heart, Christ's Home."* It describes how salvation is like inviting Jesus to come into your life just as if He is coming into your home. You invite him into the dining room, the lounge, and even into that hall cloakroom! Then you realise that the only way He can make a difference in cleaning up the house is not just as a guest but by becoming the owner. It is at that point we transfer the Title Deed to Him. He is no longer a resident but president! That's what it means to surrender to the Lordship of Christ. Jesus died on the cross, so we can die to ourselves and He can live in us.

Galatians 2:20 is describing all of this when Paul describes his life with these words "I have been crucified with Christ and I no longer live, but Christ lives in me. The life I live in the body, I live by faith in the Son of God, who loved me and gave himself for me." He was saying that the essence of the Christian life is, "Not I, but Christ living in me."

Major Ian Thomas wrote, "There are few things quite so boring as being religious, but there is nothing quite so exciting as being a Christian! Most folks have never discovered the difference between the one and the other, so that there are those who sincerely try to live a life they do not have, substituting religion for God, Christianity for Christ, and their own noble endeavours for the energy, joy, and power of the Holy Spirit. They are lamps without oil, cars without petrol, and pens without ink, baffled at their own impotence in the absence of all that alone can make man functional; for man was so engineered by God that the presence of the Creator within the creature is indispensable to His humanity."

Discovering Great Secrets

SECOND: THERE IS PROTECTION

When our heart is Christ's home, He doesn't change addresses!

In the Old Testament there was first a tabernacle and later a couple of temples in which God's glory was displayed. In the Old Testament, God had a temple for his people, and now He has a people for His temple. The physical part of us is not some piece of property belonging to the spiritual part of us. God owns the whole works. So let people see God in and through our body.

The temple of God was a place where God displayed His glory and grace and now, as a Christian our body is the temple of the Holy Spirit. It is Christ in us the hope of glory. Belonging to Jesus, he comes to dwell in our life. Therefore, the only way we could lose our salvation would be for Jesus to leave us. And He has promised that He will never leave or forsake us. That's full cover!

In the Old Testament time, God's Spirit would come and go, but when Jesus talked about sending the Holy Spirit, to represent Him, He said, "The Holy Spirit will be with you forever . . . He lives with you and shall be in you. I will not leave you as orphans; I will come to you." When we are indwelt by the risen Christ, we never need to pray, "Lord don't take your Holy Spirit from me." Christ has come to live in our heart and we are his permanent residence! Christ in us gives protection!

THIRD: THERE IS POWER

Frustration is trying to do things *for* Jesus. Fullness is allowing Jesus to live His life *through* us! Allowing Jesus to live in us doesn't make a passive person. We will find ourself working harder than ever–but we will be working in His strength and not our own.

Notice what Paul wrote about this power, "To this end I labour, struggling with all his energy, which so powerfully works in me." Which do you think will get more done, working in your energy,

Discovering Great Secrets

or in His energy? Paul refers to this secret, mysterious power again when he wrote, "It is God who works in you to will and to act according to his good purpose" (Colossians 1:29).

A frustrated person is someone who tries to obey or serve God using their own weak energy supply. To quote Major Ian Thomas again: "Godliness is NOT your capacity to imitate God, but the consequence of His capacity to reproduce Himself in you; not self-righteousness, but Christ righteousness; It is not inactivity, but Christ-activity; God in action accomplishing His purpose through human personality—never reducing man to the status of a cabbage, but exalting man to the stature of king!"

I became a Christian in my teens years, but I didn't truly discover the secret to living the Christian life until later. These words literally changed my life: CHRIST IN YOU–THE HOPE OF GLORY. Now each year it's my privilege to teach them at Torchbearer Schools in the UK and mainland Europe, the very schools that Major Thomas founded under God.

Once I began to understand that Jesus lives in me and wants to love, forgive and encourage people through me, it made a huge difference. Instead of trying to imitate the life of Jesus, which I found to be impossible, I started learning to abide in Jesus. I'm still learning, and there are many times when I try to operate in my own strength. But if I have ever been a blessing to any by what I've said, done or written, that was not me, that was Christ in me, the hope of glory.

I heard Stuart Briscoe say once he went through four stages in coming to this understanding. When he first became a Christian he said, "Oh, this is easy! All I have to do is to repent and ask Jesus to come into my heart–no problem." But then, as he began to learn what Jesus expected of him his second stage was, "Wow, this is difficult!" He found it wasn't as easy as he first thought. Stage three was when he admitted, "This is impossible!" But after that confession, he discovered the secret of Christ in you–the hope of glory and stage four is, "This is exciting!"

Discovering Great Secrets

What stage are you at now? Are you looking for something that enables you to rejoice even when you go through the toughest times of life? The answer is found in seven life changing words: Christ in you—the hope of glory.

Are you looking for the greatest secret in all the world? A secret that was hidden for many centuries? The mystery is revealed in seven powerful words: *Christ in you, the hope of glory!*

So, now we know the start-up steps to living the Christian life.

Discovering Great Secrets

Chapter 2
FRUSTRATIONS ARE NOT ALL BAD
Delays And Denials Along The Road

Three couples were discussing words.

"Let me show you something," volunteered Vern.

He picked up the phone and dialled, *"Hello, is Charlie there?"*

"No," replied a voice, "and it's gone midnight!!"

"That was irritation," reported Vern.

He dialled the same number, *"Hello is Charlie there?"*

They could hear the angry voice at the other end.

"That was annoyance." said Vern. "Now I will demonstrate frustration."

He dialled the third time and Vern asked, "Hello, this is Charlie. Have you any calls for me?"

Frustration can be very trying.   No one can make us frustrated. People have an effect on us and situations can be trying, but a state of exasperation is our own doing! We choose our reaction. We probably tell ourself, "I'm upset." And the more we reinforce the thought, the more unnerved we feel.

Affirm, "I *have* frustration."   Don't admit, "I *am* a frustrated person." We can separate ourself from the emotion. The emotion is not us. A mood affects us momentarily, but it will pass. We are in charge of our thoughts and feelings. Patience is one 'open secret' to cope with frustration and not allow it to exhaust us. God is in the business of developing that virtue in those who acknowledge Him in all of their ways.

A key frustration
Acts 16:6-11 is Luke's description of a key frustration in the apostle Paul's second missionary journey. Paul, Silas, and the newly recruited Timothy went in search of new converts to Christ in Pamphylia and regions beyond, searching for new frontiers to conquer and were frustrated in the attempt. They were used in ways they could never have planned or anticipated.

12

Discovering Great Secrets

Paul wanted to go to the Roman province of Asia, west of Pamphylia extending over the eastern coast of the Aegean Sea. He felt this was God's game plan. However, the Holy Spirit closed the door on the province of Asia. "Having been kept by the Holy Spirit from preaching the word in the province of Asia." (Acts 16:6). The Greek word expresses an action *prior* to entering Asia. The Holy Spirit made it clear that Asia was low priority. We do not know how this was expressed. Perhaps sickness frustrated Paul going. Others have surmised that resistance from the Jews made the journey indefensible. Still others have supposed direct, inner guidance from the Holy Spirit to the mind of Paul. Whether the Holy Spirit said "No" in inner feelings or outer frustrations, the result was the same; Paul was stopped before he started out for Asia.

Unanticipated frustration

With Asia's door slammed shut by the Holy Spirit, Paul led his team north to preach throughout Phrygian and Galatian territory. Unanticipated frustrations occurred all along the way. People discovered new life in the Lord Jesus Christ and churches were born. Paul's letter to the Galatians hints at the extent of this phase of the mission. But the greatest adventure in the gospel is still ahead. Further north, the team approached the border of Mysia. "They tried to enter Bithynia, but the Spirit of Jesus would not allow them to." (Acts 16:7). Here the Greek verb is a present active form, which means that, whereas the first prohibition was prior, this one was concurrent. Paul and his team wanted to go in one direction. The Lord wanted them to go in the opposite direction. Another door closed, so they travelled east to Troas on the Aegean coast.

Remember, frustrations can be the means of disappointing to re-appoint. 'During the night Paul had a vision of a man of Macedonia standing and begging him, "Come over to Macedonia and help us."' (Acts 16:9).

Discovering Great Secrets

Clear direction

Now Paul knew the uncertain 'holding pattern' was over. Here was a clear direction. The team will preach the gospel in Macedonia. The Acts account becomes first person at this point. This is the first of the "we" passages, announcing that it was at Troas that Luke himself joined Paul and his team. The term Luke uses to describe the essence of the Lord's guidance indicates that perhaps intellect and revelation had combined to make the direction unquestionably clear. "After Paul had seen the vision, we got ready at once to leave for Macedonia, concluding that God had called us to preach the gospel to them." (Acts 16:10). The word "conclude" means "to go together, to make things agree and arrive at a conclusion". That strongly suggests that the vision confirmed what God was saying to each of them. He had brought them together in this seaport. Questions like these must have been asked: "Lord what are you trying to tell us? Why the shut doors? What next? Where do you want us to go according to your limitless wisdom and plan? Macedonia?" The vision removed all doubts. The focus of the Church was fundamentally changed and incalculably released to transform the world. Europe and eventually the world mission of the Church resulted from the frustration at Mysia. G. Campbell Morgan affirms: "It is better to go to Troas with God than anywhere else without him." Because Paul went to Troas with God, he could now bring God's good news to Europe. What a wonderful frustration to his original plans! The Lord's "No" becomes part of His ultimate "Yes."

As we acknowledge our Lord in all our ways, we can depend on both reason and our inner feelings. If we have surrendered all to Him, we can dare to trust both our adverse and affirmative thoughts and feelings. There are possibilities which are not God's maximum for us if we are open to what He has planned. It was not the Lord's timing for Paul to go into Asia, although later it would be right for him to go to Ephesus on the coast of that province. The Lycus valley of the region would never be personally reached by Paul. Colossae, Laodicea and the other cities of the area would be reached later by his disciple

Discovering Great Secrets

Epaphras and would be charged by the Lord to the ardent care of the Apostle John. God gave His "No" about going into Asia at that time because He wanted to get him on to Macedonia. With hindsight, we can see that he was right.

Things I have almost done
We all know times when we feel hindered and certain directions seem to be wrong. I am awed by all the good, appealing things I have almost done in my life. Looking back, they would have been calamitous compared with the supreme things God wanted me to do. I have heard the indisputable "No!" then when I determined not to do what seemed so right by my own standards of appraisement, I turned to see a new outlook. But going in the direction in which one is guided always involves hazard. Paul and his team pressed on, taking the risk, for the Holy Spirit knew what He was doing with them. They did not decline to advance when at any point they were prohibited by the Spirit from going into Asia or Mysia; they risked moving in new directions each time. The way they had chosen was disqualified by the Lord. This got them to Troas and gave them an assurance of what they were to do.

There are times I wish the Lord would write out the instructions (in triplicate and confirmed by fax) and send them by angelic messenger (preferably an arch-angel) so that I would know what I am to do and say on every point for the rest of my life. But the Lord knows me too well to do that! He knows that I would put my trust in the teachings and not in regular daily, contact with Him. He gives me the long-range goals, certainly. I am not at all hesitant about the focal aim of my life to proclaim the gospel and be part of His Church. But for the daily decisions about precedence, He gives only as much as I need to know in order to do His will in each situation. The venture is in daring to believe that He will be resolute to give me all I need to know, say and do in the fleeting challenge or opportunity. That way I can learn from both the failures and successes. When I give the Holy Spirit a willing and open mind, alert and aware sensibility and live in constant communication, he does give me clear-sightedness, although along the road there will be surprises I never visualised. Our confidence is that God knows what He is doing; He can get through to us with His intention; our willingness makes possible this phenomenon; and He will use our obedience as occasions of growth we never imagined possible.

Paul, Silas, Luke and Timothy arrived first in Philippi where they led Lydia and her household to Christ and there established a church. (Acts 16:11-40) Paul and Silas were arrested on false charges, beaten and put into prison. God delivered them and they were able to lead the jailer and his household to faith in Christ. After encouraging the new believers, Paul and his friends left Philippi (though Luke probably stayed behind temporarily) and headed 100 miles S.W. for the important city of Thessalonica. The synagogue gave them a natural bridge for communicating the gospel. "Some of the Jews were persuaded and joined Paul and Silas, as did a large number of God-fearing Greeks and not a few prominent women" (Acts 17:4).

And so the church was born in Thessalonica.
You can visit Thessalonica today, only the travel brochure will call it Thessaloniki. (It used to be known as Salonika). It is an important industrial and commercial city in modern Greece and is second to Athens in population. The Jews of the city became so enraged by his teaching about Jesus that they created a riot and took captive Paul's host, Jason, holding him responsible for the apostle's behaviour.

From Luke's record it may appear that Paul and Silas left the city almost as soon as they arrived (Acts 17:10). I don't think so! There is ample evidence from Paul's letter to the Thessalonians that a lot of time elapsed between verses 4 and 5 in Acts 17. The team probably spent some months ministering to new believers and winning others for Christ. Paul gave in-depth teaching that would have taken a lengthy period of time (1 Thess. 2:7-10). Paul left the city, travelling south to Berea and there began to preach again. The Jews from Thessalonica, however, followed him, creating another uprising in Berea. Finally, Paul was sent on alone to Athens. He

Discovering Great Secrets

remained but a short time there and he addressed this letter to the new believers in Thessalonica. Paul is clearly the real author of the letter (cf. 2:18; 3:5; 5:27). But Silas and Timothy share his concern for the Thessalonians' spiritual growth. Silas was a member of the Jerusalem church and a Roman citizen. He replaced Barnabas as Paul's colleague on the second missionary journey (Acts 15:40). Silas was content to play second fiddle. How unlike some people, If they can't be number one they refuse to be anything else. Not so with Silas. It's never easy to take a subordinate position to a person of outstanding ability and strong personality. But one characteristic of a Christian servant is his readiness for unnoticeable service in places of secondary significance.

Timothy may still have been a teenager, perhaps 19. He joined Paul (perhaps 50 years old) at Lystra and was to become the apostle's most trusted lieutenant (Acts 16:1). When the town fathers at Thessalonica demanded Jason's guarantee that Paul's team would leave the city, they travelled to Berea, 50 miles away. More trouble stirred up the people against the missionaries, so the believers sent Paul to Athens while Timothy and Silas stayed at Berea. Paul soon sent for Timothy to join him at Athens. (Acts 17:10-15). At this time Timothy received his first solo assignment. He had been with Paul just a year or so and would have been only 20 or 21. Paul sent Timothy back to Thessalonica to strengthen and encourage the faith of the new believers. William Barclay compares Timothy to a postage stamp: "The postage stamp sticks to its job. It is stuck on the envelope and there it stays until it has reached its destination... It did not matter to Timothy where he was sent. He went. It was enough for him that Paul wanted him to go... One of the great tests of any person is if he can really put his back into the things that he does not want to do." (God's Young Church, Westminster). Timothy, Paul's understudy, had passed a major test as a trainee in his visit to Thessalonica.

So the letter to the Thessalonian Church begins. The frustrations of ministry, the strategies and plans discarded. The questioning heart, "What do we do now, Lord?" Guidance is not something we go to God to receive. It is the inner assurance, which comes from being carried along in the stream of the Holy Spirit, through the rocks and rapids of dangerous alternatives. Paul and his team were being carried by the river of the Holy Spirit. They were not so much seeking guidance as in the flow of guidance. Each decision was not an occasion to reintroduce themselves to the Spirit; rather they were swept along, given instructions and directions before and in the midst of each phase of the evolving mission. Frustration? Yes! But also surprises we never anticipated. The Gospel in Europe.

Christian ministry is going where you're sent: staying where you're put, doing as you're told, repeating what you're told and leaving when you're done. To be 'sent' means that someone else initiates their activity in your life. Someone else is responsible for that which they have initiated. Our efficiency without God's sufficiency leads to deficiency.

Let's learn from the up-and-down life 'happenings' of Paul and his team.
Being a Christian does not always make life easy. In some ways it does. After all, Jesus said, "My yoke is easy and my burden is light." (Matthew 11:30). Jesus promised, "I am with you always, to the very end of the age." (Matthew 28:20). God has said, "Never will I leave you; never will I forsake you." (Hebrews 13:5). I have had people share with me their great disappointment with God because they thought He promised them better than they got in life. When they became followers of Jesus they understood that He would answer all their prayers, solve all their problems, heal all their diseases and make life constantly happy. Then came sickness, sadness and setbacks that really hurt and took them by surprise. It is not what they thought the Christian life would be like. We must beware of the idea that the Christian life is always easy. It is not. The Christian life is good. The Christian life is supernatural. The Christian life is special. But it is not easy.

"No temptation has seized you except what is common to man" (1 Cor.10:13). There are troubles in life that are part of the

Discovering Great Secrets

universal human experience. It is part of living in our world and no one is exempt. Christians are as vulnerable to natural disasters, mental illness, financial losses and family problems as anyone else. Please don't think that because of faith in Jesus Christ as Saviour we are immunised against life. The difference is not what happens to us but how we respond to what happens. Don't get discouraged! It can be tough to be a Christian. We don't want tough times but we should not be surprised by them. On the contrary, we should consider it a privilege to belong to Jesus Christ whether life is easy or hard.

In 1914 Ernest Shackleton sailed from England with a 27-member crew aboard the Endurance headed for the largely unexplored continent of Antarctica. His biographers tell about an ad he ran in a London newspaper in anticipation of his journey: "MEN WANTED FOR HAZARDOUS JOURNEY. LOW WAGES, BITTER COLD, LONG HOURS OF COMPLETE DARKNESS. SAFE RETURN DOUBTFUL. HONOUR AND RECOGNITION IN EVENT OF SUCCESS." 5,000 men volunteered to go.

Far more than signing up with Shackleton, becoming a Christian is joining a great adventure with God. It is exhilarating, promising and spectacular but there are inevitable frustrations along the way and billions have volunteered. The Christian life is very good but don't be surprised when it is also very hard. "Dear friends, do not be surprised at the painful trial you are suffering, as though something strange were happening to you." (1 Peter 4:12) Recognising the difficulties of life God promises special provisions for followers of Jesus. "Do not lose heart. Though outwardly we are wasting away, yet inwardly we are being renewed day by day. For our light and momentary troubles are achieving for us an eternal glory that far outweighs them all. So we fix our eyes not on what is seen, but on what is unseen. For what is seen is temporary, but what is unseen is eternal" (2 Cor. 4:16-18). The point Paul is making is that the troubles and delays of life are temporary; they will pass and Christians will experience the wonder of heaven when today's troubles will be forgotten.

Discovering Great Secrets

As Christians our lives are not always easy. We experience the same universal problems of life as everyone else. We may even suffer extra pain and problems just because we are followers of Jesus. But when we do, God steps in and provides supernatural love, care, promise and strength. We get to experience God in new and deeper ways because of the problems of life. It is not that Christians have a life that is easier but that we have a God who is greater!

In December 1914 the Endurance entered the ice fields of the Weddell Sea. The pack ice froze around them and the promises of the advert started to come true: "HAZARDOUS JOURNEY. LOW WAGES, BITTER COLD, LONG HOURS OF COMPLETE DARKNESS. SAFE RETURN DOUBTFUL."
They stayed in and around the ice-locked ship for ten months. No one else in the world knew they were there. Finally the ice crushed the ship. Twenty-eight men started walking across the frozen sea, dragging three lifeboats and minimal supplies. When they reached open water they floated to Elephant Island. It seemed hopeless. Between them and South America was the Drake Passage with the roughest seas in the world. Shackleton and four crewmembers took one of the lifeboats and headed away from South America toward South Georgia Island where there was a whaling station. Without adequate navigation equipment they aimed for a speck in the Southern Atlantic Ocean that was 800 miles away. Bitter cold and dangerous waters surrounded them. They were the only hope for the 23 men left behind on Elephant Island. Shackleton was a committed Christian. He prayed for God's grace and God got them to South Georgia Island. But they landed on the wrong side. The whaling station was on the other side of a mountain range that had never been climbed by humans. Without experience or proper climbing equipment, Shackleton and two of his men headed up the mountains and over ice fields, through blizzards and over treacherous cliffs. They made it in 36 hours. Ernest Shackleton wrote in his diary: "I know that during that long and racking march of 36 hours over the unnamed mountains of South Georgia, it seemed to me often

Discovering Great Secrets

that there were four, not three. I said nothing to my companions, but afterwards Worsley said to me, 'Boss, I had a curious feeling that there was another person with us.

God did not preserve them from difficulty but he climbed their mountains by their sides. They reached the whaling station. They led the whalers back to the Antarctic Peninsula and Elephant Island where the other twenty-three crewmembers were marooned and rescued them all. Not one was lost.

God has not promised us a life of ease. He has promised us *Himself* and grace sufficient for whatever we face.

Chapter 3
GROWING UP OR SETTLING DOWN?
Sign Posts Pointing To The Right Destination

"School days are the best days of your life" some people say. I
don't agree. I looked forward to the time when mine came to an
end, even though I was an outstanding pupil. 'Outstanding' in
the corridor, and 'outstanding' in the front of the Head Teacher's
office. I detested most the end of term reports. I required a
signature from a parent acknowledging the report. At least I
didn't have the indignity of a boy in one school. The physical
growth of the boys was recorded and one boy was 5ft 4in at the
beginning of school term and 5ft 1in at the end. The
schoolteacher, not at all perturbed, wrote on his report, "settling
down nicely". This is funny when it comes to a school report,
tragic when it comes to a Christian life. We are meant to "grow
in the grace and knowledge of our Lord and Saviour Jesus
Christ". (2 Peter 3:18).

Paul needed to leave Thessalonica in a hurry, possibly after
only a few months. But he left a growing Church and he always
remembered them in his prayers, thanking God for all of them.

*'We always thank God for all of you, mentioning you in our
prayers. We continually remember before our God and Father
your work produced by faith, your labour prompted by love and
your endurance inspired by hope in our Lord Jesus Christ. For
we know, brothers loved by God, that he has chosen you,
because our gospel came to you not simply with words, but also
with power, with the Holy Spirit and with deep conviction. You
know how we lived among you for your sake. You became
imitators of us and of the Lord; in spite of severe suffering, you
welcomed the message with the joy given by the Holy Spirit.
And so you became a model to all the believers in Macedonia
and Achaia. The Lord's message rang out from you not only in
Macedonia and Achaia—your faith in God has become known
everywhere. Therefore we do not need to say anything about it,*

for they themselves report what kind of reception you gave us. They tell how you turned to God from idols to serve the living and true God and to wait for his Son from heaven, whom he raised from the dead—Jesus, who rescues us from the coming wrath.' (1 Thessalonians 1: 2-10)

QUESTION:
How far forward are we in our Christian growth?

Have we developed over the last six months? As we consider the rapid growth at Thessalonica we can evaluate our growth pattern.

What is the sign of growth?
It is not the number of people who attend church services, but the presence of three qualities. FAITH, LOVE, HOPE. In the New Testament, these are always listed as fundamental characteristics of those who have come to Christ. (Cf. Eph. 1:15-16, 18; Col 1:3-5; 2 Thess. 1:3; Phil. 1:4-5). FAITH roots us in the past and the history of Calvary. LOVE roots us in the present of our walk with God and relating to one another. HOPE takes us into the future. It is more than the wishful thinking of the kettle. Up to its neck in hot water but keeps on singing. Christian hope is firm and established.

These three are actions not attitudes. "Work produced by faith, your labour prompted by love and endurance inspired by hope" (v.3).

Have we faith that acts?
Faith that doesn't act is not faith at all. A prayer meeting was being held in an area of terrible drought. The people came to pray for rain. Just one girl brought an umbrella. Faith put into practice is the kind of faith by which growth is measured; people who are not operating from their own resources but being stretched. It has been said, "We are not saved by faith plus works, but by faith that works." Check your growth. Have you a developing, growing faith? Not a naiveté but trusting God for what may seem impossible.

Discovering Great Secrets

Have we got a love that labours?
More is said in the New Testament about love than any other quality. We use the word love so generally. "I love my wife. I love my dog. I love strawberries and cream." Is love measured primarily by how we feel? No! It is what we do, not how we feel. Of course we can feel affection and God can give us affection for others that we naturally would not have. But love is more than that. "We always thank God for a love that made you work hard," says Paul.

Have we a hope that hangs in?
'Endurance inspired by hope in our Lord Jesus Christ' (v.3). There is faith, love and plenty of hope in this world, but if the Lord Jesus Christ does not inspire it, it will not last. Hope provides patience. We are able to take a long view of things.

QUESTION:
What is the source of this growth?
PREDESTINATION, PREACHING, PRACTICE.

PREDESTINATION - "Brothers loved by God we know that he has chosen you" (v. 4). God does not do anything unless He decides to do it. The Christian life does not begin with man's decision but with God's decision for us. God does not create provisions to meet our problems. He allows problems to meet His provisions. When God created the world, Adam did not have to hold his breath until God could create some air to breathe. God provided the supply before there was a need.

Which came first, the last Adam (Jesus Christ) or the first Adam? The last Adam. Which came first, sin or salvation? Paul tells us we were chosen in Christ before the foundation of the world (Ephesians 1:4; Rev 13:8). Before there was a garden in Eden there was a cross on Calvary. God had already taken the initiative. Salvation was always in the heart of God. It was not an afterthought. He believed it was worth the risk to have an extended family for his Son Jesus Christ, in what would eventually be a new earth and a new heaven. There is no need in your life which God has not already met. "He has blessed us

Discovering Great Secrets

in the heavenly realms with every spiritual blessing in Christ" (Eph.1:3). We do not have to pray, like the little girl, "Our Father who art in heaven, how do you know my name."
We do not have to recite:
"To those of us who know the pain,
Of Valentines' that never came.
And those whose names were never called,
When choosing sides for Basketball."

We usually think of hypocrisy as someone projecting an image of being better than they actually are. However, it is as much hypocrisy to project an image of being worse than you are actually are! "We are God's workmanship created in Christ Jesus to do good works, which God prepared in advance for us to do" (Eph.2:10). Literally, His work of art. We are unique. No one has ever been made just like us. Therefore, we can offer to God something that no one else ever can.

A Tattoo Shop in Hong Kong has a standard tattoo on offer (at a discount price) 'Born To Lose'. Asked if anyone actually wants that tattoo, the answer given by the shop owner is, "Oh yes. But before tattoo on skin – tattoo on mind." Too many people have a loser attitude. "His divine power has given us everything we need for life and godliness through our knowledge of him who called us by his own glory and goodness" (2 Peter 1:3). I think that our lives will be well on the way to being transformed if we would begin each day, for thirty day, saying that out loud and asking God to help us to really believe it. There are, after all, two ways to start the day. You can begin by saying, 'Good morning, Lord' or 'Good Lord, it's morning. Begin the day reminding yourself of the kind of God He is. All that we need, we have already. It is a matter of appropriating what we have.

Every time we pray we recognise we cannot make people believe in Jesus Christ. All we can do is move them in that direction and remove some of the darkness from their thinking. When we pray, we look for the moving of a sovereign God, who by His Spirit can illuminate their thinking and start the process that will bring them life. It is God who takes the initiative and it

Discovering Great Secrets

is His love that decides those whom He will call. This is not arbitrary.

We know why God chooses. He loves to choose nobodies. If we want to see God at work look around for nobodies. God loves to seek and save that which is lost.

We know how God chooses. It was the Holy Spirit who told Paul to go to Thessalonica. "We know that God has chosen you because our Gospel came to you not simply with words, but also with power, with the Holy Spirit and deep conviction" (v 4, 5).

I can preach my heart out, try to be persuasive, reasonable, logical and technical for the appropriate people and nothing will happen. God must set the ball rolling. We don't know who God will next convert. Who would have thought that Paul, the former Saul of Tarsus, whilst breathing out threats against Christians, would have been called of God. Paul writing to the Galatians said that God "set me apart from birth", (Gal. 1:15).

God chose the main means to bring this about.

PREACHING - One of my worries today is the drop in morale about preaching. Parents can unwittingly hinder the spiritual growth of their children by saying. "Now this is going to be an adult sermon, you will not get anything out of it." Who says so? History testifies that God can take something preached and apply it deeply into the lives of boys and girls. Murray McCheyne, greatly used by the Lord in spiritual revival, tells of children coming together for prayer meetings, little boys and girls becoming evangelists. As they grew up physically, they also grew spiritually.

The revered Bible commentator Matthew Henry was converted at the age of eleven. The greatly used American theologian and scholar Jonathan Edwards was aged eight. Puritan Pastor Richard Baxter was six years old. Youth does not give God our ability but our availability.

Discovering Great Secrets

Let us get rid of phrases like "Stop preaching at me." Find another expression. Recognise the importance of presenting God's truth to people.

Two Scottish ministers were lamenting the good congregation on a Sunday morning, but a dismal one on Sunday evening. People would turn out in the morning but would not come back for Bible study on a Sunday evening. One minister commented that he had tried everything. He had even invited the local football team and the town band but the congregation did not come. Three months later he decided to close the Sunday evening service. The other minister asked, "What did your Elders say about that?" The minister replied. "They don't know I have closed it yet."

Other things are helpful but it is preaching that God uses. God has ruled out man's wisdom as a way of getting to heaven, otherwise it would be salvation by works. When God's word is proclaimed works are completely ruled out. Preaching is something we all can do. We can gossip the Gospel. But it is a certain kind of preaching which will be effective.

A story is told by Dr. Mahaffy, former provost of Trinity College Dublin. When asked by a local clergyman how he had liked his sermon, Dr. Mahaffy replied: "It was like the peace and mercy of God." The clergyman was deeply flattered and wanted to know why he was making such a sublime comparison. " Well," said Dr. Mahaffy, " it was like the peace of God because it passed all understanding and like his mercy because it showed every sign of enduring for ever." (Murray Watts, Hot under the Collar, Monarch Publications).

Question:
Why did the psalmist prefer to be a doorkeeper in the house of the Lord?
Answer:
So he could stay outside while the sermon was being preached.

Discovering Great Secrets

Some preachers don't need to put more fire in their sermons; they need to put more sermons in the fire. Paul was not an impressive orator. He didn't have an attractive way of presenting things. Legend suggests that he was bow-legged, balding and small in stature.

George Whitfield, mightily used by God had a squint. Christmas Evans, a great, anointed evangelist, had a false eye. Twenty minutes into his sermon his eye socket would fill up with moisture. He would take out the false eye, wipe the socket with a handkerchief and pop the false eye back again.

God mightily used that man. He continually uses many people whose presentation would definitely not make them television personalities with the correct sound bites. The Word of God is never out of date; it is always relevant. A man can be thoroughly sound and send his congregation sound asleep if the power of the Spirit is missing.

R T Kendal, past minister of Westminster Chapel tells a story (against himself) of memorising and preaching Jonathan Edwards famous sermon, 'Sinners in the hands of an angry God'. When Edwards delivered that address five hundred strong men were hanging onto church pillars and women were fainting. It began the great evangelical awakening. R. T. preached it. His congregation yawned. Some years later he was encouraged when he discovered that Jonathan Edwards himself, repeated that sermon and also had no impact.

"Our Gospel came to you not simply in words but also with power and with the Holy Spirit and with deep conviction." (v. 5). If we are not convicted or don't practise what we preach, we will not be able to convince anybody else and our preaching will fall to the ground.

PRACTICE - "You know how we lived among you for your sake. You became imitators of us and of the Lord" (v. 5, 6). Most things we learn are by imitation. Watch a little girl playing with her dolls imitating her mother. Watch a boy in his toy car manoeuvring so adeptly between the gateposts imitating his dad. Watch him turning backwards on two wheels screeching and bumping the lamppost – imitating his mother!

The Thessalonians imitated the evangelistic team. Despite severe suffering, they welcomed with joy the message given by the Holy Spirit. They became a model to all the believers. This tribute is high praise. Why? Because Paul gave this distinction to no other church.

"The communication of the Gospel is by seeing as well as hearing. This double strand runs through the entire Bible: image and word; vision and voice; opening the eyes of the blind; unstopping the ears of the deaf. Jesus is the Word of God. Jesus is the image of God. The Word became visible; the image became audible. Now the verbal element in evangelism is clear. Where is the visual? And the answer is: in Gospel churches, communities that are changed by the power of the Gospel." (John Stott quoting Canon Douglas Webster, The Gospel, The Spirit, The Church. S.T.L. 1978).

"A poor widow in Guatemala was down to her last twenty cents and without food. She began to pray about her problem. As she was praying, she felt a deep conviction that God was telling her to go to the large supermarket in town the next day and fill up several carts with groceries and take them to checkout stand number 7. This was not just a vague feeling on her part but a deep, Spirit-born conviction. She went to the supermarket the next morning, loaded enough groceries into carts to last two or three months and took them to Checkout 7. Just as she got there the cashier closed the stand to go out to lunch. She suggested that the woman, take her groceries to another stand, but the woman said, "No, I cannot. My Father told me to take these through checkout stand 7." So she waited while the clerk went to lunch and came back again. The clerk was surprised to see the woman still there and started to check out her groceries. Just then an announcement came over the loudspeaker: "This is our seventh year of business and we are pleased to announce that whoever is checking out at checkout stand number 7 gets free groceries!"

Discovering Great Secrets

Now I am not telling you to do what this woman did. What I am saying is that we are to believe that God cares for us, that He is a loving Heavenly Father and He has a thousand and one ways of meeting our needs but He hardly ever does the same thing twice"! (Ray Stedman, Discovery Papers 1978).

The Thessalonians demonstrated a practical faith. The message rang out around Greece and was known everywhere. The imitators were now the imitated! There was nothing left for the team to do. They could move on because those who had come to faith were gossiping the message. The commission to make disciples is not to the church, it is to the individual.

What will we do about our personal responsibility? Are we going for growth? The signs are faith, love and hope. The source is predestination, preaching and practice.

WHERE DO WE START?
Paul uses three verbs to show us three steps to take. TURN, SERVE and WAIT.

"You turned to God from idols to serve the living and true God and to wait for his Son from Heaven." (vv. 9-10). The moment we turn to God we are expressing faith. When we serve the Lord we express love. As we wait for the coming of the Lord Jesus we are expressing hope.

TURN TO GOD

The word for 'turned' in the Greek is the same word used for conversion throughout the New Testament. God cannot be seen if we have our backs to Him. We cannot hear Him if we are walking away from Him.

Notice the direction of this action: to God from idols. It is not put the other way around. You do not leave your idols for some reason and then painfully try to find God. What happens is that you discover something of the beauty and greatness of God and seeing that and wanting it, you are willing to forsake the cheap and gaudy things with which you have been trying to satisfy yourselves.

Read this carefully. We tend to think that we have to clean ourselves up first, and after we have become more spiritually presentable, then we will get serious about our faith. We have it backwards. We cannot get straightened out on our own. The issue is not improving our behaviour. It is turning to God. Clean up times come later. *"We maintain that a man is justified by faith apart from observing the law"* (Rom.3:28). The order is significant. We cannot leave our idols and then try to find God. What happens is that we discover the goodness and greatness of God as we see the changed lives of His followers. When we see it, we want it, and so we turn to God.

We may not bow down to a lump of wood, but whatever has the first place in our lives, is our idol.

Some parents idolise their children, some idolise the car. Many of us would label television as an idol. I do not think so. It is rather, an altar upon which are spread offerings and sacrifices to the great god of self. Television panders to our desire for comfort and amusement. It lures us to think always of our own comfort, our pleasure, and our fear of tedium or desire to be either enthused or frightened by watching some display or event. It encourages us to focus upon ourselves.

Our growth will begin when we turn *"to God from idols to serve the living and true God"* (v.9). The word 'serve' is the same word used for a slave. It is in the present tense to show that service is a continual activity, not a once-in-a-while action. Serving is a lifestyle.

SAVED TO SERVE

Do you feel worthless, untalented or too old? You are still breathing aren't you? If you are unsure go to the bathroom mirror and breathe on it. If a thin mist is left, you are still alive. *There is something you can do.*

Discovering Great Secrets

As a young Pastor with my 'L' plates on, I was often very direct in some of the things I would say. I would now be just as direct but I would clothe my words. On one occasion, I asked a man if he would be willing to help in a youth club. The man muttered, "I'd love to help, but I'm so worthless and undeserving." I was sorely tempted to respond, "Off course you are! If we had anybody superior, do you think we'd ask you?" That would hardly have been a tactful or Christian remark, but I am sure there are innumerable pastors who feel like doing the same thing when they face similar occurrences.

God can use imperfect persons to do His perfect will. Our service is dependent upon what God is, not what we are. Serving others is the way to achieve joy and fulfilment, as you learn to encounter God through those people whom you serve.

There is a true story of a boy who suffered under the Nazis during World War II that clearly communicates what I am trying to put into words.

'A Jewish boy was living in a small Polish village when he and all the other Jews of the vicinity were rounded up by the Nazi SS Troops and sentenced to death. This boy joined his neighbours in digging a shallow ditch for their graves. Then they were lined up against a wall and machine-gunned. Their corpses fell into the shallow grave and then the Nazis covered their crumpled bodies with dirt. But none of the bullets hit this little boy. His naked body was splattered with the blood of his parents and when they fell into the ditch, he pretended to be dead and fell on top of them. The grave was so shallow that the thin covering of dirt did not prevent air from getting through to him so that he could breathe.

Several hours later, when darkness fell, this ten-year-old boy clawed his way out of the grave. With blood and dirt caked to his little body, he made his way to the nearest house and begged for help. Recognising him as one of the Jewish boys marked for death by the SS, the woman who answered screamed at him to go away and slammed the door. He was turned away at the next house as well as at the one after that. In each case, the unwillingness to risk getting into trouble with the SS troops overpowered any feeling of compassion that these people might have had. Dirty, bloodied, and shivering, the little boy limped from one house to the next begging for somebody to help him. Then something inside seemed to guide him to say something that was very strange for a Jewish boy to say. When the next family responded to his timid knocking in the still of the night, they hear him cry, "Don't you recognise me? I am the Jesus you say you love."

After a poignant pause that must have seemed like an eternity to the little boy, the woman who stood in the doorway swept him into her arms and kissed him. From that day on, the members of that family cared for that boy as though he was one of their own.' (Tony Campolo, Who Switched the Price Tags, Word Books 1986).

The woman who took him in on that horrible night told this story. She told the story not to elicit praise for herself, but to tell others of the joy and happiness he had brought to her over the years. She had discovered that labouring to help hurting people is serving Jesus Himself. What could be more fulfilling work than that?

Have you turned to the living God? Are you serving other people for him?

WHAT ARE YOU WAITING FOR?

"Wait for his Son from heaven, whom he raised from the dead – Jesus, who rescues us from the coming wrath." (v.10). The word for "wait" occurs only here in the New Testament. It implies maintained expectancy.

An interesting feature about the Thessalonian letters is that each chapter of both letters ends with a reference to the coming of the Lord. At Christmas we look back to his first coming, but in the early church there was little mention of that. They celebrated it. But for them, they believed that he was coming again and their hope lay in that. It was the ever-present hope of the early church and hope became the ascendant theme of these Thessalonians letters.

They looked backward to the resurrection. That fact was their answer to the threat of personal death. This was their ground of confidence for conquest over death. Jesus had said, "Because I live you shall live also."

I believe the Scriptures teach that every believer at his or her death is caught up in the return of Christ: that then, for each of us, we become part of the great eternal event, which later will come rushing into time. When is Christ coming? The answer is that he is no further away than your own death. You may not be here tomorrow. If that is so, for you Christ has come; the return of Christ is accomplished. Jesus promised, "If I go and prepare a place for you, I will come back and take you to be with me that you also may be where I am" (John 14:3). What a wonderful promise. We can look back to the resurrection, where we see our victory over death assured. We can look forward to a time that Paul calls "the coming wrath". That is not hell. He is not talking about the fact that Christians are delivered from the fires of hell. John 5:24 records the words of Jesus, "Whoever hears my word and believes him who sent me has eternal life and will not be condemned; he has crossed over from death to life." (John 5:24).

The Thessalonians knew they had already learned from Paul that they would not come into that judgement. But here he is talking about a coming wrath. The use of the present tense indicates that it is something yet future. Jesus would also rescue them from that wrath.

In the Old Testament this period is called "the terrible day of the Lord". It is a time when God's judgement will come down upon the earth. Jesus himself described it as the great tribulation. That time is for the future. It was for them and still is for us. But throughout these letters we discover that God has a design to deliver His own from that "coming wrath". Christians have the

Discovering Great Secrets

advantage even over the approaching crisis of the world. Much more than the assurance of heaven, or the avoidance of the agony of living, the promise is of help right now. Interwoven with the promise of John 14 that Jesus would come again is the promise that He will come to live within us now (John 14:17-18). The wonderful paradox Christians have is that though Christ's kingdom is yet to come when Jesus returns to this earth, He is already here with us now. Even now, He is guiding us, satisfying us, protecting us. The question this raises is, what does this mean to you? Christians have no business to be discouraged, disheartened or despondent. If we yield to any of these moods, or feelings, it is because we have neglected these great truths. But there in harassed Thessalonica, those truths were to be living, alive and sweet in the hearts of those believers. God is calling us back to this again in our day of history.

Turning to the living God . . . it is far better than settling down nicely.

Discovering Great Secrets

Chapter 4
STRESSED OUT BUT STRENGTHENED
An Emotional Journey

Emotions can do some strange things. Dr. James Dobson tells of a group of tough U.S. marines dropped behind the lines during the Vietnam War. They were told, "This is a Vietcong area, hold the hill and dig in." At 1.30 that night the attack began. They fought all night long, the night sky lit up with the firepower. Early the next morning the Vietcong had withdrawn. They checked for bodies. Nobody was there. They had imagined the whole thing. Someone got nervous and fired, causing a return of fire from the other side of the camp. They fought the night – and won. Your mind will tend to conform to your emotional feelings even if the emotions are invalid.

Paul's 1 Thessalonians letter gives the inside story on his tangled emotions.

'When we were torn away from you for a short time (in person, not in thought), out of our intense longing we made every effort to see you. For we wanted to come to you – certainly. I, Paul did again and again – but Satan stopped us. For what is our hope, our joy, or the crown in which we will glory in the presence of our Lord Jesus when he comes? Is it not you? Indeed, you are our glory and joy. So when we could stand it no longer, we thought it best to be left by ourselves in Athens. We sent Timothy, who is our brother and God's fellow worker in spreading the gospel of Christ, to strengthen and encourage you in your faith, so that no one would be unsettled by these trials. You know quite well that we were destined for them. In fact, when we were with you, we kept telling you that we would be persecuted. And it turned out that way, as you well know. For this reason, when I could stand it no longer, I sent to find out about your faith. I was afraid that in some way the tempter might have tempted you and our efforts might have been useless. But Timothy has just now come to us from you and has brought good news about your faith and love. He has told us

Discovering Great Secrets

that you always have pleasant memories of us and that you long to see us, just as we also long to see you. Therefore, brothers, in all our distress and persecution we were encouraged about you because of your faith. For now we really live, since you are standing firm in the Lord. How can we thank God enough for you in return for all the joy we have in the presence of our God because of you? Night and day we pray most earnestly that we may see you again and supply what is lacking in your faith. Now may our God and Father himself and our Lord Jesus clear the way for us to come to you. May the Lord make your love increase and overflow for each other and for everyone else, just as ours does for you. May he strengthen your hearts so that you will be blameless and holy in the presence of our God and Father when our Lord Jesus comes with all his holy ones.' (1 Thessalonians 2:17-3:13)

I am so glad that Paul was honest. There were times when he was afraid. There were occasions when he was bubbling with joy.

I wonder where the idea arose that Paul was stern and cold? You cannot read this letter without sensing the warmth of his heart and the depth of his love. At the time he wrote this letter, he was ministering alone in the city of Corinth. He was feeling the loneliness of that moment. Being far away from loved ones is a very unpleasant experience. Forgetting the danger that had driven him from Thessalonica and the cruelty he had experienced there, he longed to be with them again.

Already in this chapter we have three sources of opposition to the apostle: Opposition from the state (v. 2); opposition from society (v. 14); and here, opposition from Satan. While this might look like three enemies, it is really only one. Other Scriptures indicate that the state and society are often the channels of the devil's attempt to hinder the spread of the good Word of God. This is what Paul encountered.

We sometimes get the idea that the ideal Christian life is to be beautifully even. I don't find that in the life of Jesus (John

11:35). A little girl said to her mother, "Mummy, do all fairy stories begin 'once upon a time?" "No, dear," she replied, "some begin, 'When I became a Christian I came to the end of all my troubles." How true. Becoming a Christian you did come to the end of all your troubles – this end. There are more to follow. You have simply exchanged one set of troubles for another. The difference is, you are getting all of your troubles over now with none to come in eternity, which is just when the unbelievers' will begin.

Paul is open about his stressed-out emotions. More important than his struggles are the actions he took when he experienced emotional stress.

Consider Paul's emotional temperature. Notice how it goes up and down.

HE BATTLES WITH ANXIETY

He had been in such a tense and dangerous situation he left Thessalonica quickly and quietly. Some believers were probably saying, Paul is a fly-by-night. He can't stand the heat. He has left us in our hour of need. Paul says: "We were torn away from you" (v. 17) Paul dealt with the Thessalonians with the gentleness of a mother (2:7) and with the firmness of a father (2:11). The phrase 'torn away' is a very powerful image that literally means, "When we were made orphans." Paul was a mother and father and now feels like a child who has been ripped away from his parents. Because of intense Jewish opposition, he was run out of town. His body left them but not his thoughts. His heart was still in Thessalonica. He wanted his body to return to where his heart was. Even though our hearts are with people, that is not enough. We need physical contact. Paul felt he had not said a proper goodbye and longed to return. Some of the new believers were beginning to question his motives. "If he loved us why did he leave us? And why doesn't he come back to see us again?"

Discovering Great Secrets

Paul truly had a deep love for people. He so loved the Philippian Church he said, "I desire to depart and be with Christ, which is better by far; but it is more necessary for you that I remain in the body" (Phil. 1:23-24). Love for the Corinthian Church led him to write, "I will very gladly spend for you everything I have and expend myself as well" (2 Cor. 12:15).

You know how good parents talk when away from their young children, often wondering and worrying about their welfare. "We made every effort to see you, for we wanted to come to you – certainly I, Paul did, again and again – but Satan stopped us," says Paul (1 Thess. 2:18).

The phrase, "Satan stopped us," is a military metaphor for an army that sets up a roadblock in order to impede the enemy. It can also refer to the breaking up of a road so that it becomes impassable. Every time Paul tried to return to Thessalonica he ran headlong into a satanic obstruction. I would love to know the answer to certain questions. How did he know it was Satan? How could he be so sure? Shall I tell you why Satan does this? If Satan can keep Christians apart, he will. If he can keep someone who can meet your spiritual needs away from you, he will. I don't know whether it was sickness. Perhaps it was difficulties crossing the frontiers. If Satan can stop Christians building each other up he will.

Paul has a double desire. He wanted to be present with them on earth and proud of them in heaven. That is one Christian meeting Satan cannot stop – when our Lord Jesus Christ comes. Paul wants to be proud of them then. "What is our hope, our joy, or the crown in which we will glory in the presence of our Lord Jesus Christ when he comes? Is it not you?" (v. 19).

When you face Jesus what will be your glory and joy? There are many things we purr over now that will count for nothing then. You may have passed your exams, been successful in business, bought a delightful and spacious house. In that day your glory will be the number of people brought closer to God through your witness. It was Howard Hendricks who said, "Only two things in this world are eternal – the Word of God and people. It only makes sense to build your life around those things that will last forever." Because this is true, we are wise to make sure the Bible is in us and that we are investing our lives in people. Our goal should be to go to heaven and take as many people as possible with us. Will you burst with legitimate pride in the presence of Jesus? With legitimate pride Paul says, "You are our glory and joy". That is Paul's ambition. What is yours? If you have the same desire as Paul you will understand what he says next.

IN HIS ANXIETY PAUL ALSO EXPRESSED FEELINGS OF DISTRESS.

Paul's team had gone further south to Athens. Some people say, "No news is good news". I don't think so. You tend to imagine the worst. Paul was not only interested in starting a church. He was prepared to send Timothy back to them to help their spiritual growth. Paul felt like death warmed up. He was distressed by two things:

First, that they would become discouraged.

Thank God for honest preachers who clearly state that Christianity exchanges one set of troubles for another. When Paul was with them, he kept telling that they would be persecuted (see v.4). It is one thing to know it in your head but still another when it happens to you. For every Christian, life is a battle. I have noticed that our Lord often gives a special protection to a new believer – what we might call a honeymoon period. Then he lets us live in the real world with its indifference and rejection of the Gospel. Paul is worried the believers at Thessalonica will be "unsettled by these trials" (v. 3).

Second, they would be tempted.

Satan is winning against Paul. He has been prevented from returning. When the going gets tough we can be tempted to check out. Paul was a good evangelist. He was afraid his "efforts might have been useless" (v. 5). Tough times can tempt us to give up.

Discovering Great Secrets

Paul was so worried that these new Christians would crumble that he sent Timothy to find out if they were still standing strong. Trials can cause casualties even for the most courageous of Christians. Under pressure we can develop wrong attitudes, and slide down the slippery slope of despair.

To the emotions of *anxiety* and *distress*, Paul also had more positive emotions.

A ZEST FOR LIVING

"Timothy has just come to us from you and has brought good news about your faith and love." says Paul (v.6). This is the only time the word: 'gospel' is used in the New Testament other than for the message of the Gospel of Jesus Christ. "He (Timothy) told us you always have pleasant memories of us and that you long to see us, just as we also long to see you". (v.6) Christian workers often hear about the problems and that can lower morale. But to hear someone going on in faith and love helps God's servant to know it is worthwhile after all.

Nothing is more encouraging for a Christian worker than to learn that his converts are "standing firm" (v. 8). Think now of the person most instrumental in your spiritual growth. Can you contact them?

The faithfulness of Paul's converts was a life and death matter for Paul. "For now we really live," he says (v.8). This letter must have been written as soon as Timothy had returned. If you can contact the person who has spiritually helped you, who knows – you might just put new life into them.

That sent Paul's emotions soaring.

THE WONDERFUL EMOTION HE FEELS NOW IS – JOY.
"How can we thank God enough for you in return for all the joy we have in the presence of our God because of you" (v. 9). Paul was not working up a state of pseudo-fervour. Where you do not experience profound emotion when praying, just ignore the

Discovering Great Secrets

emotion and keep praying. Paul prayed earnestly. Nothing flippant, "Bless me and my wife: son John and his wife: us four and no more". He takes time to think deeply on their needs.

Paul prays frequently.
"Night and day we pray" (v. 10). He puts it this way in 5:17, "Pray continually." Corrie Ten Boom, who was held in a concentration camp, writes this about prayer, "When a Christian shuns fellowship with other Christians, the devil smiles. When he stops reading the Bible, the devil laughs. When he stops praying, the devil shouts for joy." *(Prayer Powerpoints, Victor Books, p.109).*

While Paul is making and mending tents, his lips are not moving but his heart is communing.

Paul prays fervently.
"Night and day we pray most earnestly" (v.10). He is going above and beyond all normal measures. It can be translated, 'super abundantly'. There is no power in prayer – the power is in God not our prayers. But our prayers lay the track along which God's power can come. If we do not lay the track the effects will not be known through us. If we are casual about our praying little will be achieved. Half-hearted prayers produce half-hearted results. God says, "You will seek me and find me when you seek me with all your heart" (Jeremiah 29:13).

Paul prays specifically.
He wants to see them again (see v. 10). A Physical blockage to being with them did not prevent him from praying. Tell God exactly what it is you would like done. Some of our prayers are not answered because we are not precise enough in our requests (James 4:2).

C.S. Lewis imagines a hellish conversation in his famous Screwtape Letters, "It is, no doubt, impossible to prevent his praying for his mother. But we have the means of rendering the prayers innocuous. Make sure that they are very 'spiritual', that he is always concerned with the state of her soul and never with her rheumatism." *(Screwtape Letter, C.S. Lewis, Fontana).*

Check how specific your prayers are. Would you know when God has answered? Do you pray too generally? What helped him to keep praying? Spot my deliberate mistake: "night and day I pray most earnestly that I may see you again". It is not *'I'* (singular) but *'we'* (plural). *"We* pray most earnestly that *we* may see you again" (v.10). This is not a private prayer.

He prayed corporately
Consider what Jesus said: "This is how you should pray: 'Our Father in heaven' ." Not "My Father." It is a pagan idea to think that we can ever pray privately. We are joined with the angels of heaven every time we pray (Rev. 4:8).
What more can a group prayer meeting do? Surely, if we all pray like fury for the same thing even if we are not physically with one another, that should be enough. No! A prayer meeting is a school, fireplace and powerhouse. We learn how to pray in the company of other believers. (Luke 11:1). We help one another to keep spiritual fervour (Rom. 12:11). Corporate prayer releases greater power (Acts 4:31). Can you imagine the prayer meetings Paul, Silas and Timothy had?

Paul wants to see the Thessalonian believers again. "and supply what is lacking in your faith" (v. 10). The word he uses is used for the mending of nets (Mark 1:19). Our faith never reaches perfection; there is always need for adjustment and growth. We go "from faith to faith" (Rom. 1:17). Faith is like a muscle: it gets stronger with use.

Paul prayed to overcome satanic hindrance.
Probably five years passed before the prayer was answered. But it was answered. Have you felt like giving up on prayer? Don't. Pray some more.

Paul's request was also that their love might "increase and overflow for each other and for everyone else" (v.12). Times of trial can be times of selfishness. Persecuted people often become very self-centred and demanding. What life does to us depends on what life finds in us; and nothing reveals the true inner man like the fire of affliction. Some people build walls in times of trial and shut themselves off. Others build bridges and draw closer to the Lord and his people. This was Paul's prayer for these believers and God answered it (2 Thess. 1:3).

The entire Trinity is involved in this prayer. Paul addressed the Father and Son in verse 11. In verse 12 "the Lord" may refer to the Holy Spirit, since "our Lord" at the end of verse 13 certainly refers to Jesus Christ. If this is so, then this is the only prayer in the New Testament directed to the Holy Spirit. The Bible pattern of prayer is: to the Father, through the Son and in the Spirit.

Paul wants his converts to stand "blameless and holy in the presence of God and Father when our Lord Jesus comes with all his holy ones" (v.13). Since all believers will be transformed to be like Christ when he returns (1 John 3:2), Paul could not be referring to our personal condition in heaven. He was referring to our lives here on earth as they will be reviewed at the Judgement Seat of Christ. We will never face our sins in heaven, for they are remembered against us no more (Rom 8:1; Heb. 10:14-18). But our works will be tested and you cannot separate conduct from character.

It is time for a review.
This passage takes just a few moments to read. But what an emotional helter-skelter we ride. *Anxiety, distress, zest for living, joy, dissatisfaction.* Whatever emotions we experience now, that is nothing to what we will feel when Jesus returns.

The lessons.
There are many lessons we can learn from Paul's emotional graph in this section of his letter. Let's look at a few.

Emotional downsides are normal.
They are not wrong nor are they avoidable. Paul could not stop the trials and persecution. There are certain circumstances that

are beyond our control. Anxious feelings are therefore inevitable. For every up there comes a down. That is how we are made. It helps to roll with the blow when you acknowledge this. As you listen to a person sharing his emotions be careful to refrain from telling him how he should feel. There are no 'shoulds' or 'should nots' with feelings; they just are. You may not understand another's emotions, but don't deny or ignore them.

Don't wallow in an emotional downer.
Every anxiety and distress demands we ask what action we must take to resolve the stress. The resolution to Paul's stressed-out feeling was to send Timothy to find out what has actually happened. Some people avoid finding out what is happening in case what they fear is a reality, so they just go on worrying. Often the fear may be unjustified. And even if it is based on reality, finding out what has caused the problem often enables us to solve it and thereby overcome our fear and anxiety.

If you have pleasant memories, don't have a short memory.
Look for opportunities to show appreciation in tangible ways. Encourage one another. This is required of all Christians (1 Thess. 5:11).

In his play *Pygmalion,* George Bernard Shaw suggests that a lady and a flower girl differ not by the way they act, but by how they are treated. In My Fair Lady, the musical of Shaw's play, the delightful flower girl Eliza Doolittle expresses these sentiments after she has undergone the transformation from pauper to a much-praised lady. She contrasts the encouraging style of the sympathetic Colonel Pickering with the unyielding bantering of her tutor, Professor Henry Higgins. Then she concludes that she never ceases to be a lady around the colonel because he never fails to treat her as such, but Professor Higgins' rough treatment of her prevents her from ever fulfilling the part around him. The encouragement process provides energy to a path of improvement.

Discovering Great Secrets

When you feel low because of a 'no-go' sign, don't give up.
Some Christians are tempted to interpret all barriers to achieving difficult goals as God's barriers. "If God wanted me to accomplish this goal he would have opened the door and made it happen." If that were true, why did Paul say: "Satan stopped us" (1 Thess 2:18)? Some things are wrong. We are stupid to persevere. Some plans are right. We should set up alternative plans and persevere. God will clarify the difference when we are open to him.

Satanic opposition is permitted by God.
The book of Job says that Satan had to come before God and get permission from Him to afflict Job's body (Job 2:6). This man lost everything – his family, home and wealth. He suffered terribly from boils, which covered his whole body. But God had allowed it. The end of the book reveals what was accomplished by that suffering, but it was all hidden for the moment from Job's eyes. So too, it is hidden for our eyes, but the Bible reveals there is a malevolent power of evil at work. There are demonic beings, master manipulators that are able to lead people about, putting thoughts into their minds and planting obstacles in the path of the gospel. God permits this for this reason: these things are used by Hm.

Opposition is His method of training.
Affliction, suffering, pain and heartache are often God's way of getting our attention. Many of you have gone through that. You paid little attention to him until you suffered a time of great heartache. Then you began to hear what He was saying to you. God uses opposition to train us, not only that, to give us an opportunity to overcome trouble, to rise above it. Don't give up!

Keep praying with and for one another.
Don't settle for the status quo. Paul's prayer was answered in the affirmative, because during his third missionary journey, on his way back from Jerusalem, he did visit Macedonia again. Thomas Chalmers was right when he said that, "Prayer does not just enable us to do a greater work for God. Prayer is a

greater work for God." Paul prayed without ceasing for his loved ones in Thessalonica. Night and day!

My priorities.
I don't know about you, but the example of Paul and the mix of his emotions prompt me to evaluate my priorities. We sometimes get bogged down in the daily routine of living and forget the essential task of our life. If we begin now to allow the Spirit of God to use us to win men, women, boys and girls to faith, love and hope in the Saviour, what high emotions there will be in the presence of our God.

Discovering Great Secrets

Chapter 5
EXPECTING MORE
The Road To Recovery

More and more doctors are running their practices like assembly lines. One man walked into a doctor's clinic and the receptionist asked him what he had. He said, "Shingles." So she took down his name, address and told him to have a seat. Fifteen minutes later a nurse asked him what he had. He said, "Shingles." So she took down his height, weight, complete medical history and told him to wait in the examining room. A half-hour later another nurse came in and asked him what he had. He said, "Shingles." So she gave him a blood test and told him to wait for the doctor. When the doctor came in and asked him what he had. He said, "Shingles." The doctor said, "Where?" He said, *"Outside in the truck. Where do you want them?"*

With the best of intentions we don't always get things right! And that goes for living the Christian life as well. There is often a big gulf between what we *want* God to do and what we *get*.

Taking time to check out what Asaph in Psalm 77 discovered can be a real and relevant help. Think about it. There is a steady diet of books and testimonies explaining the amazing miracles God does. "You've got a problem? Here is God ready to help you right this very moment. All that you need do is ask in faith and it will be done." This kind of attitude is around us today. What do we do when it doesn't work out well?

Asaph was used to singing and talking about God's power. In Psalm 77 he is transparent enough to acknowledge that there came a time when he almost lost faith. The wonderful thing about his song is that he moved from perplexity to peace. From confusion to confidence. From stress to strength. I think we need a bit of that as well, don't you?

Discovering Great Secrets

Some big stress factor is beating down on Asaph and he is having sleepless nights. Do you know the feeling? He hasn't got the strength to sleep yet he's exhausted. Don't forget that Asaph is not just starting out as learner in God's school - he is a mature man of God. He is a celebrity. He leads the nation in big-time worship celebrations. Now something is wearing him out. It will sound familiar to some of us for sure - "God, if prayer doesn't work what have I got left?" He thinks about 'the former days'. He can look back on a history of God being far more exciting back then than now. This man certainly believes in God but has unanswered questions. He feels alone and neglected by God.

He is asking questions of God. Get that point – because we need to realise that we are free to question God. Jesus asked questions of God and other people. You look back on past blessings, and then you look at your 'now' situation and you say, "Why not now? Why miracles then but not now? Why help then but not now?" That is Asaph's tough reality, "God is different to what He used to be like."

In his book 'Disappointed With God', Philip Yancey writes that in Peru there is a small Indian village with a thriving fifty year old Church. Close by the building in which they worship is a granite marker. The missionary father of a six month old son is buried there. The little lad died of vomiting and diarrhoea and the father cracked up and died of hysterical diarrhoea. He gave up on the Lord. God is his goodness has built a Church where the missionary gave up.

There are three ways of approaching God: *Belief, doubt* **or** *unbelief.* Belief and unbelief are deliberate acts. We choose to believe or not to believe. We have to ask, "Have we got a reason for our belief or unbelief?" Doubt can be an honest expression. It can be a process to pass through on the way to belief. The Christian faith is true, and God is perfectly capable of doing what He wants. And we are free to ask questions, "Where can I turn? What can I do next? Where are you, God, in this mess?" Committing our life to God we expect something and we can get confused when we get nothing back. God will not knock us over the head if we ask questions.

Psalm 77 shows how Asaph found his way from confusion to confidence. Don't we want to travel the same route? Let me underline. It's not unusual to go through times of trauma, testing and trial. This appears to be God's standard programme for training us.

Have you noticed that in the Bible Jesus usually turns up about four days late to help? When his friend Lazarus died that's what He did. The two sisters of Lazarus couldn't take this in, "If only you had been here our brother wouldn't have died." 'If only' – how often we find ourselves in an 'if only'. "Where were you, Jesus?" Do you know what was happening here? Mary and Martha were looking for a *restoration* from bad health. Jesus was looking for a *resurrection* from death. As David Pawson says – *"To have a resurrection you have to let Lazarus die!"* There are many situations we can find ourselves in where we are looking for God to step in and make it better and to do it right now. And God says, "It's going to get worse before it gets better, because I want to do something much bigger and better."

Asaph is asking questions and doubting. Suddenly in verse 10 there's a big change. "Then I thought, 'To this I will appeal: the years of the right hand of the Most High.' I will remember the deeds of the Lord; yes, I will remember your miracles of long ago. I will meditate on all your works and consider all your mighty deeds." Instead of struggle and uncertainty, there is security, and confidence starts to grow.

I find three questions come out of what I read.
First: WHAT STARTED HIM ON THE ROAD TO RECOVERY?
Second: WHAT KEPT HIM ON THAT ROAD?
Third: WHY DID GOD LET HIM STRUGGLE IN THE FIRST PLACE?

Discovering Great Secrets

When we get hold of the answer to this it will be an incredible help for those times when God seems to have gone on holiday and we need Him the most.

QUESTION ONE:
WHAT STARTED HIM ON THE ROAD TO RECOVERY?

Why is he unsettled and then begins to become re-assured? The answer is, he saw where he was heading and he stopped. Thinking that God could forget him he realised that the next step would be to say that "There is no God to remember me at all." And he knew he didn't want to go down that cul-de-sac. A very good thing to do in a time of uncertainty is to look at the end of the road we are on. I've found it helpful to say when someone has come to me unsettled about what to think or believe, "Are you able to do without God?" The answer is 'No.' Why? Because we're battling with insecurity right now but it will become worse if we walk away from God.

The apostle Peter understood this. Many left Jesus because they didn't like what he was saying. Jesus turned to his disciples and asked, "Are you going to leave Me as well?" Peter said, "Where will we go?" In other words, he had been thinking about it. However, he knew that if he walked away he would be walking away from what really mattered in life. And that's how Asaph is feeling.

So, having stopped himself from an overreaction we come to the second question we need to ask: How did Asaph move on from this point? Many Christians stop the drift but don't take the *couple of steps* Asaph now takes. What happens? They remain believers but never get a depth to their faith.

QUESTION TWO:
WHAT KEPT HIM ON THE ROAD?

We get the answer from verse 11, "I *will* remember the deeds of the Lord; yes, I *will* remember your miracles of long ago. I *will* meditate on all your works and consider all your mighty deeds."

51

Discovering Great Secrets

With the crucial words, *"I will"* he caught hold of himself. He's no longer the victim of his feelings. His mind comes into the picture.

The first step is this:
THINKING BEFORE PRAYING.

His troubles launched him into prayer, "Lord I'm in a mess, help me out." It was wrapped up in self-pity. What is wrong beginning with our self? We have a limited horizon.
There was a movie where one character stepped out of the movie screen into the real world and was shocked. When he was hit it hurt. When he kissed he felt. Then he climbed back onto the screen and tried to explain that to the rest of the characters, but they couldn't take it in. How could they? Their horizon on life wasn't big enough to understand. That's why we need to stop and think because we get locked into one dimension.

Let's say that the help we need is with our physical health - the way to operate is to move from *thinking* to *prayer,* not the reverse.

Think about God, and then pray with confidence. Of course. Guard against wrong thinking about God. Before you can build a house you must demolish the old building. So, let's knock down any old ideas that have been built in our minds, doing us no good.

Here are five ways of thinking that must go.

Wrong Thinking Number 1:
BE HEALED BY FAITH, DON'T TAKE YOUR MEDICINE.

Never ditch subscribed medication, unless you're a hypochondriac where it's self-subscribed and there may be some good reason for doing it. Do you realise that you don't have to make a choice between God and science? Receive prayer and keep taking the tablets.

Discovering Great Secrets

Wrong Thinking Number 2:
THE RIGHT FORMULA GUARANTEES SUCCESS.
Jesus didn't have a fixed formula in prayer. There were times when He would touch a needy person. But at other times He would work at a distance. He might use spittle or He might use mud, or nothing at all but His word. Don't get fooled into thinking that there's a right method. "If you can just say it and do it the right way the healing will come." *Think before you pray.*

Wrong Idea Number 3:
WHEN IT DOESN'T WORK, BLAME SOMEONE.

Some people will say to you, "More miracles happen in the developing world than here." And then blame the western church for its lack of faith. Maybe their faith is greater. Perhaps God is merciful because of their lack of medical provision. God's works of *supernatural healing* are wonderful. God's gifts of *medical science* are equally wonderful. Reliable results can come from both means. It's all a gift from God.

Wrong Idea Number 4:
I HAVE THE POWER.

God used Peter and Paul in spectacular ways. But they never tried to draw attention to themselves. "Look what we can do. 3 o'clock tomorrow there'll be another series of miracles for you to see." They realised that the power was in God not them. Don't focus on the one praying but on the One in whose name your prayers are prayed.

Wrong Idea Number 5:
BLAME THE DEVIL.

Here we must watch out for two extremes. *One:* A Sunday morning only religion. We only think about God then. *Two:* Seeing demons behind every sneeze and cough.

Discovering Great Secrets

There is a balance to reach in our thinking. What is right thinking? What ideas should we starting building in our minds?

Right Thinking Number 1:
HEALING IS KNOWN ALONGSIDE SUFFERING.

This is demonstrated in the Cross of Jesus. He did miracles and still suffered. We note this truth in the troubles of the apostle Paul. He did miracles in the name of Christ but suffered terribly. There were times when he feared for the life of a friend. To claim that healing must always happen will lead some people to pretend it has when it hasn't. Others will feel a false guilt because surely they should have the faith to get better. Other people will become cynical about the whole subject. Still others will go on an endless quest for *Reverend Doctor Always Right* to come along with the formula that will heal.

Right Thinking Number 2:
HEALING CAN MAKE SUFFERING HARDER.

There is a puzzle here which we must acknowledge. Hebrews 11 lists Old Testament heroes of faith. People helped, rescued, successful, because of their faith in a God able to deliver them. Check out the end of the chapter and do you know what you find? People commended for their strong faith who struggled, were persecuted, suffered and died. It says that all these lived by faith. The writer notes something about this group that it doesn't of the former group, *"Of whom the world was not worthy."* As if God was saying, "They're too good for planet earth. I want them to be with me where I am."

God is not at our beck and call to do just as we decide but as He decides. Healing speaks of dying well and not never dying. There will always be extremes. We must watch out that we don't fall off either side of the wall. We can fall down on one side by never praying for supernatural healing. That is wrong. We can fall on the other side by thinking that total healing is promised in the Bible for right now. Naive idealism leads us into unreality. Weary cynicism will box God in. God will give us 'tasters' of His deliverance in the here and now. The main blessing is when we are part of His new earth and new heaven. When we have a body just like the body of Jesus.

Like Asaph – First, we need to do some **THINKING BEFORE PRAYING.**
SECONDLY: WE NEED GOD'S WORDS BEFORE WORKS.

Just as we don't start with prayer but with thinking. We don't start with words but with God's works. God's words are very helpful to build us up. But our faith must rest upon the actions of God. Even at the human level, what a person *does* speaks so loudly we can't hear what they *say*.

We see this step that Asaph takes throughout Scripture. When John the Baptist was in a dungeon and unsure about his future, he lost the plot for a moment. He sent a message to Jesus to ask if He really was the Messiah or should they be looking for someone else. He had his doubts. How did Jesus respond? Did he get upset with John, "What a display of small faith, of course I'm the Messiah. You should know that, John." No. He didn't give him words He gave him deeds. "Go back and tell John what is happening. The blind seeing. The disabled walking. The deaf hearing. Tell him these deeds because he knows the Old Testament Scriptures predicting that this is what the Messiah will do when he comes." Thomas doubted Jesus was back from the dead. What did Jesus do? He showed Himself to Thomas: "Look at the nail print in my hands. Look at the scar on my side." This was more than words. It was deeds. It was actions.

God's works strengthen our faith because they give us objective evidence. If our faith is resting upon emotional feelings within us we will remain unsettled because those feelings can change. Actions are timeless. Actions are facts that remain in history. This is a major reason for the weakness of many a believer when a trial hits them. We haven't thought about the solid events - what God has done in our past.

Discovering Great Secrets

The crossing of the Red Sea was the event which released Asaph. That had happened years before his time. Asaph sees in this God-activity the powerful control of God over all that happens. Coming to Moses the nation said, "You've led us out of Egypt but for what? Are we going to die here? You've led us to disaster. We've got the waters in front of us and the vast army of Pharoah coming up fast behind us. It's all over for us. It's hopeless. We're dead meat."

How many times have we said, "This situation is hopeless. I'm finished. There's no escape." We hit the panic button and cry out to God but at first nothing much seems to happen. But then God intervened. He got the people through the sea and stopped the Pharoah's army from following them. As Asaph looks back to that incredible action of God he realises, "I have the same God! He's no different. This is my God right now!" Behind every event that frightened Israel was God's Hand.

A magnificent example of this is Jesus before Pilate. The Governor said, "Don't you realise that I've got the power of life and death over you? I just have to say the word and it's all over for you. What do you think of that then?" And Jesus calmly replied (in effect) "You haven't got any power over me that hasn't been given to you by my Father."

Our inability to understand how God is doing things is no sign He is not doing something. I wish there were some way to impart this understanding. Often we insist that God explain Himself to us. Spell out every move that He is making just as He makes it. He didn't do that at the Red Sea but He brought them through it. Can I ask you to look back and see how God has brought you through some impossible circumstance. That action of God back then can help you now if you'll think it through. It can steady you. It can give you firm ground on which to stand.

All this brings us to the third question we want to ask.
WHY DID GOD LET HIM STRUGGLE IN THE FIRST PLACE?

Discovering Great Secrets

When a parent wants their child to walk, you know the routine. You see the 'toddler', well, named! Left foot forward followed by the left foot forward and down they go. As the child begins to get the hang of it, the parent starts to edge away. That baby doesn't know what to make of this. Why are they edging away from me rather than toward me? We know the answer don't we? They don't want to spend the rest of their life pushing the pram!

Do you know what happens when a baby Giraffe is born? A Zoo Keeper explained this. The baby comes out of the mother front hoofs and head first. If you think we human beings are in for a shock when they dangle us upside down and slap us to make us cry, well, that's nothing compared to what happened with the Giraffe. The baby falls about ten feet landing on its back. The mother looks around for a minute and then kicks the baby. She wants it to get up, you see. She then gives it another kick, because she wants it to remember how it got up that first time. If God instantly responded to every need just as we had a need, we would depend upon our feelings for everything.

As Asaph thinks about that Red Sea incident he realised it was God's intention to lead them through the waters. This was His intention when they left Egypt, "Your path led through the sea, your way through the mighty waters."That never entered their minds, but God knew it. Though His 'footprints were not seen' – that is they couldn't predict how things would work out – God knew all along what He would do.

God's path leads **through** the sea, **through** the trouble and not around it. Remember Asaph's circumstance – he's cried out to God and sees no hope. He didn't hear God answer. Remember Israel was up against the Red Sea with the Egyptian army behind them. They were desperate. Like Asaph, they had seen God work in their past. The plagues had just come, showing God's power, holiness, and redemptive love for them. Instead they got caught up in their present circumstances and present emotions and didn't see God working to save them.

Discovering Great Secrets

Moses' response to the people was, "Stand by and see the salvation of the Lord which he will accomplish for you today!" This is Moses speaking to the people. The very next verse in Exodus 14 is fascinating. Moses must have been pleading to God in a similar fashion to Asaph. Moses was standing firm in front of the people and encouraging them, but clearly before God he had the same attitude as Asaph. God speaks to Moses, saying "Why are you crying out to me? Tell the sons of Israel, go forward!"

The Israelites were afraid of the Egyptians, but they were also afraid of the sea. They couldn't walk into the sea - that was death for them. Yet what does it say about the waters? "When the waters saw you, O God, *they* were afraid." He gives a personality to the water to make an important point. The very thing that makes us frightened is in its turn afraid of God. Anything we face in this world that causes us to fear is under the control of a sovereign God. Whatever we fear also fears God.

Notice this: "The clouds poured out water; the skies thundered; *your* arrows flashed on every side." The lightning itself belongs to God! "The crash of *your* thunder was in the whirlwind." God was in control of all of these powers that were bringing fright to the people. The people didn't see this ahead of time. They saw a barrier. There was no way forward. But God's way for them was right *through* the sea. "Your path, through the mighty waters; yet your footprints were unseen." They couldn't tell that this was God's way. God was working *in* the circumstances that were causing them pain and sorrow. They couldn't see God's footprint in all this, yet He was going to lead them right through the middle of this turbulence, right through this difficulty, to a tremendous victory.

LET'S STEP BACK AND THINK ABOUT OURSELVES.

These emotions and feelings of being ignored by God. These feelings that God isn't answering our prayers, *will* come. If we haven't experienced them, I can promise you that we will at some point in our life, probably at many points.

Was God there for this Psalmist? Yes! Absolutely! Definitely! All night long while he was calling out, God was with him, God was right there! But, for his own sovereign purposes, God chose not to remove that sense of insecurity, that emotion from Asaph. Maybe he needed to learn to rely on God when the circumstances didn't make trust easy.

God's way is frequently *through* the sea, through the trial that toughens us up. We see that in in David, Jeremiah, Daniel, Paul, Elijah, in Jesus himself. How will we respond the next time? When we learn to trust God in all circumstances we will not be led astray by a promise of health, wealth, and security once we go through some religious experience. Our relationship with God like our relationships with our spouse, is not one of going through a ceremony and then living happily ever after. But like marriage our relationship to God will have its ups and downs. It will have its low and its high points.

God is always there, despite our feelings; that's what we can depend on. We need to hold onto His past works. But the emotions will come -- sometimes caused by what we ate for dinner, sometimes caused by the tragedies that accompany life in this world. The emotions will come. Asaph is telling us that we need not be controlled by those emotions. When we are faced with this, we need to recollect the solid rock of God's faithfulness, and to know that even when we don't sense His presence, even when we don't feel His love, He is there.

Do we feel like giving up on God? Hold it for a moment! God's plans are not stopped by anything in our circumstances. The smart thing is to keep trusting. Think about the works of God in our life.

Remember the greatest deed is what Jesus did on the Cross for us? We can look back to that incredible and amazing work of God toward us. If ever we want to know does God care.

Discovering Great Secrets

Does He love us? We find it displayed right there. It's a love that loves us to the end and because of the Cross there need be no end.

Tim Hansel lives in pain ever since a mountaineering accident. In the early days of his disability someone sent him a plaque with the words inscribed on it: *"Tim, trust me, I have everything under control! Jesus!"* The glass got broken in transit. He has kept it that way.

He writes, *"It speaks louder than words that way.* It is fully worth risking our life on Christ."

Discovering Great Secrets

Chapter 6
DON'T MISS THE JOY
Cul-de-sacs And Side-Tracks

Something is often missing from today's Church. It isn't that we are not trying hard or that we do not care about God and what He wants, but there is sometimes a problem and at various times in my life I have thought that I had found the answer.

I began my ministry preaching and teaching a lot about **DEDICATION**. My sincere belief was that if we had more dedicated people – people sold out to the Lord – all would go well in the church. I helped a lot of people to move forward in commitment and surrender – and that was good. But – I still sensed that there was something missing.

I started to focus on **MISSIONS**. If I could just get people to be better witnesses for Christ it would solve the problem. If people were prepared to go or prepared to support others to go out into all the world to preach the gospel it would help. I've seen a lot of people get into witness and ministry and make a difference in the lives of people who needed Christ - and that was good. But – I still sensed that there was something missing. I watched a movement emerge which spoke of 'Signs and Wonders' and encouraged us to look for the miraculous and supernatural intervention of our God. I've seen what can't be explained at the natural level. But – I still sensed that there was something missing. Don't misunderstand me – I still want to see dedicated believers. I still want to see people spreading the message of Christ. And of course I long to see the miraculous interventions of God – we all do, when we pray for the will of God in heaven to be done down here on earth.

However, I now know that we can sincerely go after many things that are good things, but still miss a vital thing in the living of a worthwhile Christian life.

Discovering Great Secrets

THE KEY ELEMENT IS JOY!

I know that the apostle Paul felt the same way because in verse 15 in Galatians 4 he asks the question, "What has happened to your joy?" And JOY can be lost! I've heard people recite Bible verses such as, "Rejoice in the Lord always", while looking as though their rich uncle has just died and left his vast fortune to his pet parrot!

There are leisure centres, sports centres, and there are 'guilt centres'! Do you know where to find a 'guilt' centre? Visit some Churches! Who are the guilt carriers who tend to leave a grim, joyless atmosphere behind them? According to Paul, they are the 'LEGALISTS'. Is there such a thing as a joyful legalist? I don't mean a legalist can't laugh, or that they have no happiness in life. They can talk, claim and act as though they have joy. But they are unlikely to be truly joyful. Joy and legalism appear to be incompatible.

The Apostle Paul addresses this issue in Galatians 4:12 to 20. Paul is asking, in effect, "What happened since we last met? We were close friends and now you treat me as the enemy. You received the truth but now you're getting into wrong ideas. I went through birth pains to help you come to new birth, and now I find myself in labour pains all over again trying to keep you from the grip of these false teachers."

The issue Paul raises that I want us to focus on is the question in verse 15: "What has happened to all your joy?" That is a huge question to think about. If we once had joy and lost it, we should be asking, "What happened to it?" God didn't take it away and old age doesn't decay it. Circumstances don't ruin it. But wrong ideas and beliefs do. Wrong ways of THINKING had come along and robbed the Galatian believers of the joy they once had.

Now let me start our thinking process with this concept:
JOY IS THE FRUIT OF THE SPIRIT, AND GOD INTENDED FOR US TO BE FULL OF JOY.

Discovering Great Secrets

"The fruit of the Spirit is love, JOY, peace, patience, kindness, goodness, faithfulness, gentleness and self-control." When the Holy Spirit controls us joy will be on show. If the Spirit is not in control, joy will be absent. JOY'S counterfeit is HAPPINESS. Happiness is directly related to the circumstances of life. When things go well, we're happy. When things do not go well, we're not happy. It's as straightforward as that. No one is happy with poverty, rejection, illness or loneliness. Pleasant times can be transitory or even totally elusive. If we equate happiness with joy, then we will perceive of the joy of the Lord in the same way. Sometimes we have it; sometimes we don't but that isn't what Jesus had in mind when He prayed for His disciples in John 17:13. He said, "I am on my way to you now, Father, but I say these things while I am still in the world, so that my disciples may have the full measure of my joy within them. I have given them Your word and the world has hated them, for they are not of the world any more than I am of the world."

Obviously joy and happiness are not the same, for in the same breath He prays for the full measure of joy for His disciples and acknowledges that the world hates them.

Being hated and happy at the same time are hardly compatible ideas. Joy must be something different. Perhaps one of the keys to understanding it is in the little word "my" in Jesus' prayer. He prayed that they might have "the full measure of my joy within them." The joy He wants us to have is His own joy, the kind He experienced when He was upon the earth.

What was that like? Fortunately, we are not left to guess concerning the nature of His joy. In Hebrews 12 the writer says, "Let us fix our eyes on Jesus, the author and perfecter of our faith, who for the joy set before him endured the cross, scorning its shame, and sat down at the right hand of the throne of God." The joy Jesus experienced was something set before Him by the Father. It was a prize promised at the end of the road–so desirable that it enabled him to endure all sorts of difficulty, pain, and even shame in order to reach it.

Discovering Great Secrets

You've heard of the term "delayed gratification" as opposed to "instant gratification." Delayed gratification is not a popular concept today. Children generally don't have the foggiest notion of what it means; teens understand it but hate it; and many adults pay it lip service only. Delayed gratification is waiting for something until you need it or can afford it, believing that greater gratification will result from waiting. It is waiting to enjoy the pleasures of intimacy until marriage, believing that greater gratification will result from waiting. Delayed gratification is accepting delays in getting what we want in the belief that getting it in God's time will make it all the better.

That's what Jesus did. He endured the Cross, despising the shame, knowing that joy and glory were awaiting Him. He could have called 10,000 angels to rescue Him from His enemies, but He knew the cross had to precede the crown. It was the end result, the goal, and the finishing line that kept Him focused. Serious athletes understand this principle. Olympic runners, for instance, will subject themselves to rigorous workouts, painful experiences, and severe deprivations in order to do their very best in the Olympic Games. They are not masochists who simply enjoy pain. They are driven by a vision of the glory awaiting them if they win the race and receive a medal. There are no shortcuts, and the process becomes endurable because it contributes to the joy of winning.

THAT IS THE ESSENCE OF THE JOY OF THE LORD.

It is a wonderful sense of privilege and an incredible sense of destiny as we participate in the grand work of Christ upon the earth. It's the expectation that the result of all our service, trials, and suffering in the cause of Christ will be a magnificent sharing with Him in His kingdom. We will reign with Him, we will sit with Him on His throne, and we will share with Him in His glory. Can anything beat that? Paul put it this way in Romans 8:18, "I consider that our present sufferings are not worth comparing with the glory that will be revealed in us." And Peter said the same thing: "Do not be surprised at the painful trial you are suffering, as though something strange were happening to you. But rejoice that you participate in the sufferings of Christ, so that you may be overjoyed when his glory is revealed" (1 Peter 4:12).

Can you begin to see why legalists don't have joy? Legalism by its very nature is focused on the journey, not the destination. The legalist is so concerned about the schedule, and whether he has the right directions, whether the suitcase contains everything needed for the trip, and whether he has confirmed reservations at a hotel for each night along the way. He's constantly complaining about the other drivers on the road who are speeding (more than he is). He has no freedom or sense of adventure. No ability to stop along the way to smell the flowers. No freedom to change the schedule. The grace-focused person aims for the destination and that makes joy possible.

Joy is the fruit of the Spirit, and God intended us to be full of it. There's nothing like the joy of first realising one's sins are forgiven. Paul hints that the Galatian believers experienced that joy when he first shared the Gospel with them and this is inherent in the question he asks, "What has happened to all your joy?" But he also talks of other qualities that accompanied their joy.

TENDERNESS and JOY go together.

Paul writes: "You have done me no wrong." He is referring to the many months he spent ministering to them. They had met his needs, received his message, and obeyed his Gospel. They had not wronged him in any way. He's making a contrast between their former behaviour and their present attitude. But the fact is, it's not unusual for new converts to treat the one who led them to Christ this way. He says in verse 13, "As you know, it was because of an illness that I first preached the gospel to you." Possibly Paul was an epileptic and that the higher, dryer climate of North Galatia was better for him than the humid coastal plain he had been working in. Perhaps he may have caught malaria in the lowlands and travelled north to recuperate.

At any rate he goes on to say, "Even though my illness was a trial to you, you did not treat me with contempt or scorn." Paul was not a great 'looker'. There are a number of comments in his letters which indicate that he was a short, ugly, half-blind Jew with an illness that made him socially unattractive. But they were so overjoyed to hear the good news of salvation that they were willing to overlook all those things.

THANKFULNESS and JOY go together.

"You welcomed me as if I were an angel of God, as if I were Christ Jesus himself." I've never had anyone mistake me for an angel – SUPERMAN yes! It's a long story – the short version is I was preaching for a week at a Church in South London. Over the entrance was a big banner – "Come and hear our Superman!" That was me folks! A one and only time that banner was used – and that's for sure! I wasn't really mistaken for anyone but myself of course. I've certainly never been mistaken for an angel - but I have had people whom I have led to Christ express their gratitude in ways that were almost embarrassing. Maybe you have had the same delight in leading someone to salvation and have experienced the same gratitude.

THOUGHTFULNESS and JOY go together.

Paul writes, "I can testify that, if you could have done so, you would have torn out your eyes and given them to me."

Actually, there may be more here than meets the eye (if you'll pardon the pun). There is evidence that the Apostle Paul suffered from severe eye trouble, perhaps a result of the blinding light he saw in his Damascus Road experience. One of the hints comes from Galatians 6:11 he writes, "See with what large letters I am writing to you with my own hand." Normally he would dictate his letters and they would be written by a secretary but when possible he would write the final paragraph by himself, although he was forced to write large. If indeed Paul did have an eye disease, his assertion that the Galatians would have plucked out their eyes and given them to him, if possible, demonstrates how much they had appreciated him and his ministry. Their joy led them to a spirit of generosity and great sacrifice.

You know, a joyful believer is a tender, thankful, thoughtful believer. Do we see all three of these characteristics to a large extent in our Church? Much more important – are they in us? Random acts of graciousness are frequent, gratitude for the message is evident, and our generosity is legendary. This to me is an indication of a high degree of Christian joy.

But while joy from tenderness, thankfulness and thoughtfulness are common marks in those who have been newly forgiven and made part of God's family, the remainder of this passage indicates that JOY evaporates when LEGALISM gets a grip on a believer's life.

"WHAT HAS HAPPENED TO ALL YOUR JOY?" Paul asks. And he follows by revealing some symptoms often seen when we toy with legalism.

HERE ARE THE SYMPTOMS OF LEGALISM.

First: We make enemies of genuine people.
In verse 16 Paul writes: "Have I now become your enemy by telling you the truth?"

I shared a Bible Conference with a committed legalist. I was teaching some really radical ideas, like the fact that God loves everyone and that taking a walk on a Sunday afternoon wasn't sinful. It wasn't disrespectful to talk to God without saying Thee and Thou. It wasn't long before I came to be viewed as beyond redemption. If we live, practice, and preach grace we will elicit one of two reactions: people will love us or hate us. They will either revel in the freedom we are offering them or they will consider that freedom a tremendous danger.

Discovering Great Secrets

Second: We make friends of false people.
Paul warns the Galatian believers about the Judaizers. Legalists are very susceptible to control by manipulative teachers. Why? Because legalism is all about control and security. The legalist is uncomfortable with loose ends and as a consequence he gravitates to teachers who are dogmatic and for whom all the issues are black and white.

Third: We make barriers to our joy.
The problem of the legalists is that they spread guilt all around the place. GUILT and JOY can't co-exist. If it's real guilt over real issues in our lives then that's a good thing. But if it's false guilt over unreal issues in our lives, then it's a bad thing.

What is Paul's answer to this tragic turnabout he sees among his converts? The treatment prescribed is a strong dose of UNCOMPROMISING TRUTH, UNCONDITIONAL LOVE and UNINHIBITED CHOICE. The Galatians were like so many whose enthusiasm for a Bible teacher wanes as soon as he delves into a subject that offends or convicts them. They like to be selective in their acceptance of truth. But the truth is the truth, and if the truth produces conflict, so be it.

The world tells us the way to resolve conflict is to compromise, and indeed sometimes it is, but not in respect to essentials. Though Paul desperately wants to see his former relationship with the Galatians restored, he is not about to compromise his convictions to achieve it. He's not about to say, "Oh, this isn't such a big deal after all; just don't let your legalism get out of hand." That would be to compromise the Gospel and to admit he was wrong in teaching in the first place that grace is the only way to God.

The mark of a real friend is that he tells those he loves the truth, even though it may cost him. Abraham Lincoln said to one of his friends before delivering a controversial address, "If it is decreed that I should go down because of this speech, then let me go down linked to the truth." That would sound pretty shocking coming from one of the front-runners for a top political

Discovering Great Secrets

job today, wouldn't it? But that's how God wants us to respond when the truth is at stake.

The only restriction God has placed upon the speaking of the truth is that it must be spoken in love. Uncompromising truth must be accompanied by unconditional love. He says in verse 19, "My dear children, for whom I am again in the pains of childbirth until Christ is formed in you, how I wish I could be with you now and change my tone, because I am perplexed about you!"

People need to know they are loved; they need to be encouraged; they need to be affirmed. A Pastor must be a shepherd as well as a teacher. The Apostle places infinite value upon the Galatians, just as a mother does upon her children. You see, Paul was their spiritual parent. He was the one who laboured to bring them the knowledge of Christ, which eventually resulted in a new birth for them. But a miscarriage had occurred along the way, and now he is in labour all over again "until Christ is formed in you," or, as one paraphrase expresses it, "until you take the shape of Christ."

Here's the BIG question –
WHAT HAS HAPPENED TO ALL OUR JOY?

Jesus prayed that we, his followers would experience the "FULL measure of JOY within us." Christ's coming to the world to forgive and coming to live His life in us by the Holy Spirit is a big change. Let's affirm it together. Let's allow our minds to absorb the fact that it means we make an uninhibited choice. In other words, CHOOSE JOY!

When we came into God's family, God celebrated.
Our reward is great in heaven.
Any trouble we have is crafting us to be like Jesus.
The joy of the Lord is our strength.
Nothing can separate us from the love of God.
The fruit of the Spirit is joy.

Discovering Great Secrets

At any moment, Jesus Himself may return. Then it really gets to be fun!

DON'T MISS THE JOY!

Discovering Great Secrets

Chapter 7
STAND FIRM AND STAY FREE
Keeping To The Main Road

The joke is told about a businessman who boards an airplane to find that his neighbour in first class is a parrot. They take off and the stewardess asks what they would like to drink. "I'll have a lemonade," says the parrot. The businessman also orders a drink. After waiting two or three minutes, the bird starts yelling, "Where's my drink?! Stop fooling around and give me my drink!" The stewardess runs to him with his glass, leaving the businessman still thirsty. Half an hour later the stewardess makes a second round. The bird orders another lemonade and a Wall Street Journal. The businessman asks again for his drink. Again, after waiting a couple of minutes, the bird screams, squawking, "Are you lazy or stupid? I want my drink, and don't forget my paper!" The poor stewardess nearly trips over herself getting the parrot his drink and the newspaper. The businessman still has nothing, and after ten more minutes he decides to take his cue from the bird. "Hey! Bring me my drink right now!" he shouts. Out of nowhere the stewardess, the captain and two passengers grab the businessman and the bird, open the hatch and throw them out of the plane. At 30,000 feet, the two are falling side by side. The parrot says to the terrified man, "Wow - that took a lot of guts for someone with no wings!"

It takes more courage for some people to do some things than it does others. For example, it doesn't take a lot of courage for me to get up and preach Jesus as the Christ on Sunday morning. The worst consequence I face is a person falling asleep. It has been said that if all the people who sleep in church on a Sunday were placed side by side . . . they would be a lot more comfortable!

There are those in the world, though, at this very moment who face very tough consequences for churchgoing. That's why Hebrews told about some of the trials faced by the saints of the

71

Discovering Great Secrets

Old Testament: "Others were tortured and refused to accept their freedom so they could be raised from the dead to a better life."

Act anyway

Someone has said, "Courage is simply the willingness to be afraid and act anyway." Very possibly there is something which God is calling us to do that scares us to death. May we be blessed with the courage we need to act anyway. My prayer is that the opening words of Galatians 5 will really help us.

A preacher took the same text, John 3:16, every Sunday for five consecutive years and never preached the same sermon. Well, virtually every paragraph of Paul's letter from the first verse has employed a different way of saying the same thing, namely that we are saved by believing, not by achieving.

Paul has brought together plenty of arguments against the 'legalists' who had gained a 'hearing' in the churches of Galatia – churches which he had established on his first missionary journey but just as we are not to grow tired in well-doing, so we should not grow tired of hearing the truth. The Bible never repeats itself without a good reason. If Paul takes most of five chapters to make his point, it's probably because we need it before the point sinks in.

Galatians 5 is important.

Notice the strange repetition in verse 1 -- "Christ set us free for freedom." And then he says the same thing negatively to make sure we don't miss the point: "Do not let yourselves become slaves again."

Why does Paul go to such lengths to stress the importance of maintaining the freedom we have in Christ? Simply because it is so easily surrendered. We are prone to letting the heavy yoke be placed back on our shoulders. We can be seduced by any number of different voices. Religious leaders may charge that we are not living up to the "real" Christian standard; the world tells us we are worthless; friends tell us we disappoint them;

parents say they will love us if we do better; spouses point out our faults and withhold their affection. When we hear these voices, we immediately are tempted to engage the work-ethic engine that insists, "I can do it; I can do it. I think I can; I think I can." We put our necks back in the yoke and try to earn approval through performance, placing ourselves under law once more. Paul sees this as a very real danger and he urges us to stand firm and resist with all our might. We must not buy into the notion that we have to win acceptance with God or anyone else by means of our performance. We must remind ourselves daily that Christ has set us free for freedom.

CONSIDER THE RIGOURS OF LEGALISM.

First: Christ will be of no worth.
The particular legalistic issue he focuses on is circumcision. If he were writing in our day I believe he would use some other issue. No one I know of is teaching salvation by circumcision today, but there are plenty teaching salvation by good character, salvation by church membership, or salvation by social activism. These things in and of themselves will not render Christ of no value; in fact, they are all good things which Christ Himself urged His followers to pursue. But if they are viewed as means of salvation, then that changes everything. Good deeds can actually keep you away from God; so can anything else that is added to the sacrifice Christ made. That addition is tantamount to denying the sufficiency of His death.

Secondly: Law will be very demanding.
The favourite theme of the legalists was circumcision, but circumcision was just one small part of the Law of Moses. There is no logical way seeking salvation by Law can stop with circumcision. To be consistent he also has to keep the dietary laws, the ceremonial laws, the tithing laws, the religious feasts, the laws on dress, the laws about how to treat certain animals, etc. Break one link in a chain and the whole chain is broken. It's no good a thief saying, "But I've been kind to my mother-in-law, and I haven't kicked the cat once this week." He's broken a law. And it's no good saying, "Oh I've been baptised" if you don't

Discovering Great Secrets

love God with all your being. A mirror with just one crack is still a broken mirror. We do not have the authority to pick and choose among God's laws.

Whenever passages such as this are read, some people immediately want to know whether they teach that a person can lose his salvation. The same question arises automatically out of the fourth consequence, mentioned in the final phrase in verse 4.

Thirdly: Grace will be lost.
Is Paul saying a person can be saved by grace and then fall away from grace and lose his salvation? I think we make a mistake when we take every passage that is difficult to reconcile with one of our favourite doctrines (in this case, the doctrine of eternal security) and massage it until it fits. Wouldn't it be better for us to admit the awful, dire consequences of legalistic Christianity and to shudder at even the thought of trying to contribute to our own salvation? That's what this passage ought to do for us.

What is 'grace'? The well-known definition is excellent – G. R. A. C. E. –
GOD'S RICHES AT CHRIST'S EXPENSE.

But 'grace' is also God's action for now. John Piper (Desiring God Ministries) has another way of understanding it built on G.R.A.C.E. – *GOD'S RESCUING AND CARING EXERTION.*

In 1 Corinthians 15:10 Paul writes, "I worked harder – yet not I, but the GRACE of God that was with me." Romans 5:21, "As sin reigned in death, so also GRACE might reign through righteousness to bring eternal life through Jesus Christ our Lord."

Grace is like a powerful king exerting His reign over us and we can lose God's special help in our lives when we start thinking Christianity is what we do FOR Him rather than what He has done in and through us.

Discovering Great Secrets

Having laid these four heavy consequences upon us, the Apostle, in verses 5 and 6, contrasts the lifestyle of the person who lives by grace with the lifestyle of the legalist. "But by faith we eagerly await through the Spirit the righteousness for which we hope. For in Christ Jesus neither circumcision nor uncircumcision has any value. The only thing that counts is faith expressing itself through love."

Paul is saying through these verses that while personal effort to become a Christian is hopeless and counterproductive, effort as a Christian is very useful, so long as it isn't geared toward earning God's favour or exalting oneself.

All effort in the Christian life (if legalism is to be avoided) must be tempered by four factors: THE HOLY SPIRIT, FAITH, HOPE, and LOVE.

Any effort that isn't generated by, motivated by, and exhibited through these four elements is almost inevitably going to lead to legalism.

The HOLY SPIRIT is the One who motivates all positive effort in the Christian life. Do you see the words in verse 5, "through the Spirit"?

FAITH is another factor. Romans 14:23 teaches that "everything that does not come from faith is sin." Abraham and Sarah were weak in faith and decided to use human effort to achieve God's promise. The result was Ishmael, the father of the Arab people. In a sense the reason we've had that horrible mess over in the Middle East for the past 50 years is that Abraham didn't allow faith to take precedence over work. But when he and Sarah allowed faith to have precedence, their efforts became very productive. Whenever faith works, great things are accomplished, the world is shaken at its foundations, and God's power is evident.

Then there is HOPE; verse 5 again: "But by faith we eagerly await through the Spirit the righteousness for which we hope."

75

Discovering Great Secrets

"Hope" in the Bible always refers to that which, though certain, is not yet fully realized. It's a synonym for "confidence." Complete righteousness will never be realised here; we must wait for it with confidence until we are ushered into eternity with Christ in heaven. In the meantime, we do not imagine we can earn it by keeping the law or practicing religious rituals. And finally, there is love. Ultimately whether one is circumcised or baptized is not the issue. What is the issue is whether his faith is a faith that expresses itself in love – love for God and love for his fellow-believer.

In verses 7 to 12 the Apostle comes back to the legalistic heresy and indicates by his own example that every effort must be made to rescue those who are in danger of falling from grace.

The tone of this section is one of strong persuasion. Paul is eager, in one last noble effort, to move the Galatians away from the brink of disaster. "You were running a good race. Who cut in on you and kept you from obeying the truth?"

The Galatians had had a good beginning in their Christian experience. They had shown signs of growth and maturity. Then something had gone terribly wrong. Someone had cut in on them. One can picture a highway scene in which one driver cuts off another and sends his car into the ditch; or a scene on the slopes in which one careless skier cuts off another and sends him into the trees. Ultimately the one who did this to the Galatians was Satan, working, of course, through the false teachers. One thing is sure. Their legalism did not originate from God. Verse 8: "That kind of persuasion does not come from the One who calls you." Legalists are great at God-talk, but their doctrine does not come from Him.

CONSIDER THE RESULTS OF LEGALISM.

There is a tragic Result for the Church.
Paul says that, "A little yeast works through the whole batch of dough." Yeast is almost always a symbol of evil in the

Scriptures. Its main characteristic is that it spreads and permeates. So does false teaching, especially, legalism. The principal point here may be that the spirit of legalism does not suddenly overpower a church. Like yeast it is introduced secretly, it grows silently, and before long it poisons the whole assembly.

Then there is a Result for the Counterfeiters.
There is a warning that "The one who is throwing you into confusion will pay the penalty, whoever he may be." Just because evil is spreading doesn't mean God will permit it to triumph ultimately. Fortunately we don't have to assume responsibility for the judgment of the false teachers—God will deal with them.

There is even a Result on the Cross.
In verse 11 we read that "the offence of the cross has been abolished." That may sound like a positive thing, but it's not. When the offence of the cross is removed, so is its power. Paul seems to be dealing with an accusation from the Judaizers that he too preached circumcision. Paul did so at one time, of course, in his pre-Damascus days. He even encouraged his half-Gentile colleague Timothy to be circumcised so that he might have a more fruitful ministry among the Jews—an action that was twisted to mean far more than Paul intended. But whatever the source of the rumour, he certainly didn't preach circumcision anymore and to prove the point he asks, "If I am still preaching circumcision, why am I still being persecuted?"

There are so many churches that mention the cross now and then, but it's so watered down, it doesn't offend anyone. You see, to preach circumcision is to tell sinners they can save themselves by their own efforts; to preach Christ crucified is to tell them they cannot and only Christ can save them through the cross. The message of circumcision (or any other kind of legalism) exalts human effort and is therefore generally popular; the message of Christ crucified leaves no room at all for human pride, and thus is generally unpopular. People hate to be told they can be saved only at the foot of the cross, and anyone who tells them so will face opposition.

CONSIDER THE RUIN FROM LEGALISM.

"As for those agitators, I wish they would go the whole way and emasculate themselves!" In effect he expresses the desire that these false teachers, who loved to use the knife in circumcision, would let the knife slip so they would be rendered unable to reproduce themselves. I admit, it may seem nasty for Paul to say such a thing, but what we must realise is that he is dealing with a very nasty heresy. Better to offend the sensibilities of his audience than to see them follow these heretics into a Christ-less eternity.

I wonder if Paul were speaking today whether he might say something like this: "Would that those who preach salvation by works, would just work themselves to death." To many in our day Paul's expression sounds coarse but he didn't speak out of ill temper. He spoke out of a concern for the truth of the Gospel of grace.

I agree with Charles Swindoll who once said, "Often we don't get angry enough about the right things." Some people blow a gasket when they hear of someone abusing animals and yet yawn when told that millions of babies have their lives snuffed out every year in our nation through abortion. Some are scandalised when a tree is cut down but shrug at thousands of people killed each year by drunk drivers. We in the church can get all bent out of shape over a Bible teacher who is too Calvinistic, too charismatic, too dispensational, or even too wordy, but we hardly pay attention as to whether or not he's a legalist.

Are we enjoying our freedom in Christ?
Will we resist having it stolen from us? It cannot be taken for granted; it must be vigorously defended. Make Jesus your final answer and the gates of heaven will swing open for you.

Discovering Great Secrets

Chapter 8
IS IT WORTH THE EFFORT?
There's Still One More Move

Every Christian at some time questions what they believe. Those who say that they don't are either dishonest or thick. It takes only a few brain cells to realise that there are many things that happen in life which contradict a breezy attitude to our faith. The only faith immune from doubt is *blind faith,* which deserves being named as a *crutch.* Real faith isn't blind and doesn't shut its eyes. It can't. It must deal with reality to be real. I'm bound to have someone reading my words who is asking right now, "Have I been wasting my life being a Christian? Is it worth it? There is no better example of this than Psalm 73. The writer has almost slipped. Life has crumbled away for him. Life has handed him a raw deal. We look at the question asked by Asaph in verse 25, *"Whom have I in heaven but you?"*

That question comes riding on the back of a great frustration in verse 11. The psalmist is looking around at people who have little or no time for God and yet seem to have an easier life than those who give God place. "They say, 'How can God know? Does the Most High have knowledge?'" The implication is, "No, He is indifferent.

It's the kind of comment you might hear in a Rugby changing room. Just off to the bar the player says, "Oh, come on, get off the God stuff. You don't really believe God is in control, do you? My life is fine as it is. Get a life. C'mon and party with us, holy man. Life is short."

In Psalm 73 the writer had nearly lost his foothold. This was no ordinary person we're talking about here, oh no! It was Asaph, the worship leader for King David. The great composer. He could take David's poetry and put it to music and do a brilliant job with it. They were memorable tunes that a nation enjoyed singing. This is one of his own poems set to music and it is pretty tough stuff. He is taking a hard look at life and not liking what he sees. But, his testimony at the end is stronger than ever. "I will tell of all your deeds" he says about God.

What we can do is trace the process from *giving up* to *going on.* Probably every week he led congregations in songs. "Let's bring our praise to our Lord people. He is worthy, Amen? Amen! Surely God is good to Israel, to those who are pure in heart. Let's sing it out."

Taking stock he LOOKS AROUND.

His experience didn't square up with the songs. He sees arrogant people in better shape than he is. They were "proud, arrogant, carefree and indifferent to God" but it didn't seem to create a cloud of gloom over their heads. In the first half of his song Asaph hits on 3 things regarding these people. Their *prosperity, pride* and *popularity.* Asaph is left asking, "Is it worth it? This God business, what's the point?" Do you know what I like about this man? He doesn't shy away from honesty.

Many of our prayers are pointless because we pretend with God. If your boss at work says, "How are you?" You may say, "Fine thanks," because he doesn't want to know your problems. But it's silly to do that with God. He does want to know. In fact, He does know.

My sympathies go out to the little boy overlooked for a prize at school. His mother said, "It's an unjust world. Virtue is triumphant only in theatricals." It appears that way. I remember seeing an episode of the TV Quiz 'Weakest Link'. One of the competitors was a Vicar. In one round he didn't do at all well. The sarcasm of the quiz-mistress just oozed, "Has God gone on holiday?" I guess you have to expect that if you go in for such a quiz. But when you feel it's true in real life, that's hard to take.

You may say, "Okay, it's a problem but what's new? This kind of thing has been happening from our school playground days. Why should Asaph suddenly get upset because there are people around indifferent to God and without struggles; their bodies healthy and strong, proud, callous hearts, conceited, malicious, always carefree, they increase in wealth?" Verse 13 answers that.

He's **LOOKED OUT** at these people but now he's looking *within* at himself. He's wondering whether keeping himself in God's good books has been in vain. He says in verse 14, "All day long I have been plagued; I have been punished every morning." The French have a saying: "We are strong enough to bare the ills of *others*. How true! It's our *own* maladies that really get to us. You will understand what the person was getting at who said, "The smallest pain in my little finger creates more mental anguish than the destruction of thousands of people I see on the TV news." We know it shouldn't be like that but it often is. And when Asaph was *personally* touched he lost his foothold. I read of children killed in war and I get upset. Something should be done. However, if it was my children I would get much more upset. It's tough being unemployed. It would be tougher if it was me! Obviously something has brought all of this home to Asaph.

What added to Asaph's problems was that he doesn't want to become a stumbling block to anyone else. 'If I had said, "I will speak thus," I would have betrayed this generation of your children' (v.15). We ought to think twice before we give voice to problems. It could damage the people around you who look to you for support.

Are your sympathies with Asaph? Is a raw deal eating away at you right now? Are you struggling with life not being fair? Have you pushed those angry feelings so far down that you deny they even exist? Or have you already turned from God because you have suffered wrongs, perhaps at the hands of Christians, and now you question, as Asaph did, God's goodness, character, and faithfulness.

Let me make this utterly clear. You're not an unbeliever because you talk like this. D*oubt* isn't the opposite of *faith*. That's confusing *unbelief* with *doubt*. *Doubt* can only be experienced by a *believer*. You can only doubt what you believe. When an atheist doubts he starts thinking that God might be there after all! Like the little boy who says to his atheistic parents, "Do you think God knows we *don't* believe in Him?" Atheists don't feel disappointment in God because they expect nothing. Those who commit their lives to God expect something and therefore are confused when things don't work out as expected. Asaph didn't cease to believe because of his uncertainties. What he went through actually contributed to his eventual stronger faith. Honestly confronting your doubts doesn't have to weaken your faith. It can make it stronger.

Had Asaph not struggled, he wouldn't have gone to God – at least not with the same desperate searching that we see here. And had he not gone to God like that, he (and we) wouldn't have come to grow so deeply in our understanding of who God is and what life is really all about.

You know, that is just like us. Almost all of us have a harder time passionately seeking God when everything is easy. And throughout all generations, it has often been in the times of testing – in the fire – that we have grown in ways we never could have dreamed.

Asaph has been **LOOKING OUT** at others doing pretty well without God. He's been **LOOKING INWARD** at himself feeling punished every morning.

Asaph found the answer from verse 17 as he LOOKS UP to God.

Problems like Asaph's are a sign we need a proper perspective. A lot of our problems arise because we stop the crime movie before it's over. Or we only read half the book and don't get to the last chapter. We can trace the **4 steps** that Asaph takes that brings help to him. I'm going to give them to you built on the letters of the word **HELP** – *H. E. L. P.* so that you can remember this and let it meets your needs now and in the future when facing a raw deal.

The first word is HOUSE.

Discovering Great Secrets

Asaph's real turning point came when he "entered the sanctuary of God." He went into God's house. Our turning point will come as we meet with fellow believers as a church. I thank God that He has ordained that we meet with others. The writer to the Hebrews knew that things were getting tough for believers in his day. He urged them not to neglect meeting together. Yes, keep the habit of joining with one another. That's the place where you get encouragement and support. Have you noticed how many times Scripture includes the will? There are times when we feel we can't worship because we're in a bad mood. We can't afford to have our worship directed by our emotions.

Asaph somehow found his way to the **'HOUSE'** of God and that's where he began to find help. The same will be true of us. Just looking around at other believers can put strength into us. They've been through the mill. They've struggled, they still do. But they're going on. That can help. We can bare one another's burdens. We can inspire one another. This isn't the whole thing but it is a vital step.

The next word is END.
"I entered the sanctuary of God (that's the **HOUSE** of God) then I understood their final destiny." Taking the short term, you would say, "Going God's way is a waste of time and effort. You come off better without him." Take the long term and you see things completely differently. Didn't Jesus say a similar thing in the Sermon on the Mount? Get on the narrow way and you limit your luggage, you limit the kind of company you can enjoy and things that you can do. It's the broad way that gives you plenty of space to take a lot of luggage with you and widen out your company. The difference is the end of the road. One leads to life the other to destruction. As a believer you are getting all of your troubles over now with none to come in eternity, which is just when the unbeliever's will start.

Two women were chatting at a bus stop about a neighbour's death. "How much did he leave?" asked one. The other replied, *"Everything!"* You have a bad dream but you laugh when you wake up. It was just a dream not real and lasting. That's how God sees the prosperity of the wicked.

"As a DREAM when one awakes, so when you arise, O Lord, you will despise them as fantasies." Success and failure must be put in its proper perspective. Once Asaph came to the **'HOUSE'** of God and met with other believers. Once he got the bigger perspective and saw the **'END'** for those indifferent to God. Well, he wouldn't want to change places with them for anything.

The next thing that helped him was that he 'LEARNED' something.

Asaph didn't just feel better he says, "I understood their final destiny." If our religion only reaches our feelings it's not good enough. There are many ways of forgetting your troubles. You can lose yourself in a movie, watch television, get a good book. And of course people will drown their sorrows in alcohol. The question is: "do they give understanding?"

There can be a false comfort in singing spiritual songs in church. It could be little different from a sing song at the local pub! We just lose ourselves in the emotions but we don't think about what we're doing.

"I'm a Christian in my way,
How? It's difficult to say.
I've the haziest sort of notion
What I mean by my devotion.
Clichés clutter up my head,
Catchwords are my daily bread.
Exquisitely undefined,
Is the thing I call my mind."

That just about sums up the approach of some Churchgoers. Never forget that the message of the Bible is to the mind. One of the satisfying things about Christianity is that we have a reason for our hope. I had to smile when I saw the Peanuts cartoon; that is, until the point went home. Linus says, "I love nature, people, birds, fish, plant life. I love without reservation: I love without thinking." We can be so like that. We don't take time to think. Going to the sanctuary of God for Asaph wasn't just a shot in the arm. A nice escapism from the real world outside.

It was a place to engage Asaph's mind as well as his emotions. It was a place to think about his God and how he related to Him. It was the place to do some relating. This can be hard work. Do it properly and you may go home from church more tired than when you arrived!

"I entered the sanctuary of God" says Asaph, "then I *understood* their final destiny." He also saw what led to his problem had been self-induced. He had built a mole hill into a mountain. I've done this and so have you: we let our feelings dominate us. We don't let the facts of our big eternal God grip our thinking. That's why a regular habit of coming to church is good. Once in a place of worship we see ourselves as we really are. As Asaph says to God in verse 22, "I was senseless and ignorant; I was a brute beast before you." Asaph probably never battled with this particular problem again because he worked it through.

HELP for doubts comes as we go to God's **HOUSE** and meet with fellow believers. Don't give up on that. We see the **END** for those full of themselves. Asaph thought that he was in a slippery place. Now from that stand point of eternity he sees that they are on 'slippery ground'. How suddenly everything can change. He has **LEARNED** something. Because he's getting his thinking round his faith and realising God's plans are bigger than a few years of success now. He is getting some sense into his attitude.

The final thing Asaph does that HELPS is PRAISE God.

Outside the house of God he thought God was being unfair to him. Inside God's house he's PRAISING and that gets him focused on real and lasting values. "Yet I am always with you;

you hold me by my right hand." People often say: "Just hold on to the Lord." I'm grateful that my relationship isn't dependent on my grip of His hand but His grip of my hand. When you cross the road with a child they hold your hand. But really it's your grip on them that counts.

Asaph goes on to say, "You guide me with your counsel, and afterward you will take me into glory." One day you may pay off your mortgage. You may get a better car. So what! I pity people investing only in such things. It won't last forever and nor will they. Every car will go to its last rusting place! All you can say is that with the price of current funerals, I'm glad to be alive!

Asaph's envy is gone. "Whom have I in heaven but you, I desire nothing on earth. My flesh and my heart may fail, but God is the strength of my heart and my portion forever." He has fallen in love with God again because he's got a proper focus.

As a Church Pastor I prepared many people for marriage. I would talk to them about 'communication'. You will have a *"Marital Adjustment Discussion"*. Which is a nice acronym to avoid having to say we're M.A.D. *'mad'* with each other. Sometimes when you're in the midst of a conflict and disagreement (A Marital Adjustment Discussion) the more wrong you are, the more you think he/she is. And if deep, deep down you know that you're wrong, sometimes you'll try and come up with 10 million reasons why he/she is actually the problem. I add, "There will probably be times when you won't want to talk." They look at me as if to say, "Not us! Other people yes, probably, but we're different." And do you know something? They prove it to me as they leave to go their separate ways. I hear them saying, "I'll text you on the way home." For goodness sake, they've been together all day. What have they got to say that hasn't been said? But of course that's how it is. Perhaps you know only too well that you can lose the talking side of the relationship in a marriage. It can drift out in your spiritual relationship as well. It must not!

Discovering Great Secrets

When we love God our questions don't disappear. They may remain with us to our last day. However, they can and must be set in a better context. With God's people - in his **HOUSE** - Putting what you see now in the wider context - seeing the **END** of people with little or next to no time for God - for the Christian, death is just a change of address. Using our minds to work and thinking about our faith – **LEARNING** - And bringing our **PRAISE** to Him because we know that He holds our hands, will guide us and afterwards take us to glory.

Look at how Asaph finished his song. 'Other people may cynically say, "How can God know? Does the Most High have knowledge."' By the end of Psalm 73, Asaph is no longer fuming about getting a raw deal. "Those who are far from you will perish; you destroy all who are unfaithful to you. But as for me, it is good to be NEAR GOD. I have made the sovereign Lord my refuge; I will tell of all your deeds."

Philip Yancey tells a personal story. He was looking through a large box of photos kept by his mother, He saw one that was of him as a baby. It was all crumpled and mangled. That was because his dad had polio and the photo had been stuck on the machine that was keeping him alive. It was right where his dad could see the picture and pray for his son. Yancey said that when he saw the picture and how crumpled it was. His mind raced back to how it must have been for his dad looking at the picture of his young son, loving him, unable to reach out to him. But *someone* who really loved was watching him! Someone who really loves us is watching us too! And that one is the Sovereign Lord. He really is our refuge.

Don't run away from your doubts.

Never yield to the school boy definition of 'faith' as 'believing in something that you know isn't true'. That's nonsense. Compelling myself to believe is no part of true religion. We don't give up the quest for truth and become Christians. There's nothing 'unspiritual' about doubts. Learn from Asaph. Look doubt in the face with a better perspective and be stronger because of it.

If you are not sure about what you believe - don't run away from your faith.

I'm not denying you have got problems about Christianity. I don't say sweep all your doubts under a mental carpet. But your doubts are not the only things you've got. Like Asaph, when you go to a church or listen to a Bible based programme on radio, you are left with a nagging thought that there could be something in this. I say, don't run away from your faith.

You say, "I need proof." What do you mean, scientific proof? Do you think you can put God in a test tube and run experiments on Him? Of course you can't. Can you measure 'right' with a ruler? Can you measure 'love' with a volt meter? You know that you can't. The answer to doubt isn't to be less honest but more honest. It's not knowing God exists but experiencing Him for yourself. Take one step toward God and He will take a dozen toward you. This is more than good advice, you can bank on it.

I love the story I heard in a recorded message by Bishop Ken Ulmer, the pastor of a church in Los Angeles, USA. He told about two men who were in an art museum looking at a painting of a chess game. One character looked like a man; the other character looked a lot like the Devil. The man is down to his last piece on the chessboard. The title of the painting is Checkmate. One of the two men looking at this painting was an international chess champion, and something about the painting intrigued him. He began to study it. He became so engrossed that the man with him grew impatient and asked him what he was doing. He said, "There's something about this painting that bothers me, and I want to study it for a little while. You go ahead and wander around." He studied it. His head started nodding, and his hands started moving. When his friend came back, he said, "We have to locate the man who painted this picture and tell him that either he has to change the picture, or he has to change the title. I have determined that there is something

Discovering Great Secrets

wrong with this painting." His friend asked, "What's wrong with the painting?" The man said, "Well, it's titled Checkmate, but the title is wrong. The painter's either got to change the painting or change the title, because the King still has one more move."

Just so you're not confused, this is the Good News: *The King still has one more move.*

A little boy named David's up against the giant named Goliath. David is in trouble. He tries to put on King Saul's armour, but Saul's a 52-Long, and David's a 36-Short. He can't even handle a grown-up's sword. It looks like Checkmate, but... *The King still has one more move.*

A man named Daniel gets thrown into a den of lions, because he refuses to stop praying to his God. The lions are hungry. He's in there all night. At the first light of dawn, Darius calls down. Daniel tells him that the lions have been put on a "Low Protein Diet," and he's fine, because... *The King still has one more move.*

A man named Moses convinces a nation of oppressed slaves to run away from the most powerful man on earth. Pharaoh sets out after them. They're standing on the shore with the Red Sea in front of them and the greatest army in the world behind them, and the people say to Moses, "Moses, what were you thinking?" And Moses says to God, "God, what were You thinking?" But *The King still has one more move!*

Going down to Judea to see Lazarus cost Jesus His life, as He knew it would. And on Good Friday, they tried Him and judged Him; they whipped Him and beat Him; they mocked Him and scorned Him; they hung Him on a cross to die and laid Him low in a tomb to rot the way every human body has rotted ever since death entered this sorry, dark world. And then they said to everybody, That's all, folks. Show's over. Time to go home. Checkmate. But they were wrong, because... *The King still had one more move!*

Discovering Great Secrets

I don't know what challenge you face. Maybe there is stress at work. Maybe you're in a marriage that is falling apart, or that has already fallen. Maybe there is a son or daughter, somebody that you love, who is struggling or estranged from you. Maybe you have financial pressures. Maybe you have done the wrong thing, or said the wrong thing, or made a mistake that feels so big it could never be redeemed.

Maybe not. Maybe things are going pretty well, and there is no crisis at all. But there will be one day. The mortality rate is still hovering right around 100%. Whatever you face, whether it's today or tomorrow, the promise of Jesus to everyone who puts their trust in Him in this, there is hope, even when it feels like "Checkmate." That's not all folks, because – as Asaph came to know in the great question he asked and answered – "Whom have I in heaven but you? . . . I have made the Sovereign Lord my refuge."

THE KING STILL HAS ONE MORE MOVE.

Chapter 9
IT DOESN'T HAVE TO BE DULL
No More Monotony For The Journey

I am disturbed by the large number of times I hear the question, "Why are so many Christians dull? What makes so many churches boring? Why is church work often drudgery rather than a delight? Put more positively, "How can I keep my faith aflame and not settle for the mundane I sense in so many Christians and experience in most churches?"

It's astonishing to realise how few people are finding life today an exciting adventure. Shouldn't we be able to expect that Christians are fascinating, and not dull people? Believing all we do, why is Christianity a drudgery of dullness for so many? How do you keep your faith from becoming stuck in the ruts of routine?

"Dull" is a many-sided word.
This makes it all the more distressing when applied to Christians. A cutting edge gone blunt has lost its sharpness and is dull. A listless, unresponsive, gormless person is dull. A person without passion in their personality is dull. A dull sound is one that is indistinct, muffled and unclear. What a word to find so easily applied to the things of God! Honest realism causes us to affirm that dullness is a word that can too readily be applied to many labelled 'Christian.'

What about us? Too many Christians have Christianity a little bit like you can get a headache. You don't want to lose your head, but you would like to lose the ache! We don't want to lose our faith, but if only it was not so boring.

How does it happen?
Sometime the dullness can be blamed on the lack of power in the pulpit. As evangelist D. L. Moody used to say, "The best way to revive a church is to build a fire in the pulpit." Other times it is the church leadership who have lost their spiritual

direction. Often the problem is programmes which maintain traditions rather than love people and help them worship and witness in the world. It is healthy for us to ask, "Why do we do what we do, the way we do it?" Jude's Epistle is almost entirely governed by a description of men that had crept into the church and were spoiling it. Much of the epistle is devoted to exhorting the true believer. The apostates had made Christianity one thing. Jude intends that his readers should show its true light in contrast to them. They were Jude's "dear friends" because they were God's dear friends. The joy of ultimate friendship with Christ must be renewed each day. We will drift back into dullness unless we experience a freshness for each day's needs and opportunities. We will become tired of the most elaborate buildings, music, and activities unless we've experienced a liberating fellowship with the Life Himself. Life in Christ is the thrilling alternative to dullness.

Jude explains the three steps to overcome the uninspiring.

(1) BY BUILDING.

"Build yourself up in your most holy faith" says Jude. We are not asked to originate faith but to build upon it. The foundation has been laid, the Apostles' doctrine. People don't see foundations, it is the building that catches your eye. It is an undeniable part of God's plan for us that we will be bored until we are involved with Him in His central work in history. He created us to know Him and build ourselves up in our holy faith. The test of faith is what you are prepared to stake on the One you say you trust. How much will we risk? Live in our own strength within the confines of our own capacities and we will never start our building programme for faith. There needs to be some area or relationship in our lives in which we are attempting the humanly impossible. Robert Browning was right: *"A man's reach must exceed his grasp, or what's a heaven for?"*

What are we reaching for that exceeds our grasp? What are we attempting that cannot be pulled off without a mighty intervention and invasion of the Holy Spirit's power? We all need a bit of danger, if we are to build our faith and win against dullness. What have we got to lose?

When my two daughters were quite young, I used to play a game with them called "play faith." I got them to stand with their back to me and said, "Right, I am going to make you a promise. Shut your eyes, fall backwards and I will catch you." So my little girls would fall over like a plank - and I caught them. An act of faith on my bare words of promise. Actually, there was a time when I failed to catch one of them. I cringe when I think of it. Happily she was unhurt, but a little reticent to trust her daddy to play that game again. But we have a Heavenly Father who will never fail us. What risks will you take on Him? Maybe because we are not prepared to take a stretching commitment to do the impossible for Christ we become drab. We lean rather than learn. We like the security. We do not build ourselves up in our faith by trying to "work it up."

You will remember the White Queen in 'Alice through the looking glass,' who said to Alice, "Why, sometimes I've believed as many as six impossible things before breakfast!" Christian faith isn't that impossible. Faith which is built on feelings is resting on a very weak foundation. Christian faith is a response to God's self-revelation. Therefore, faith fostered by prayer is strengthened by the study of the Word, and is fulfilled by our daily surrender to the Lord Jesus Himself. Faith is best built by 'one-priority' people. Those who seek first Jesus Christ's kingdom.

Be honest now. Examine our life and see what our priorities are. Are we putting God first? Or are we giving Him the left - overs? Have we let our life get so cluttered that we hardly have the time for Him anymore? That's what a lot of believers do. They are not living in sin. In fact, they are trying to follow God, but they have filled their lives with so many activities that they can't spend time in the Word or prayer. Don't let that happen to you. Simplify your life. Shed all those things you cannot afford spiritually. Get rid of those seemingly harmless activities that drain your time and energy. Let nothing crowd God out of first place. When you start parcelling out your time, put Him first and keep Him there day after day!

If we don't give Him the priority everything else in our lives will be doomed to failure because without Him whatever we do will lead to nothing. Jesus said that Himself (John 15:5;). The Bible doesn't teach us we can be born again and then float along. If we want to build spiritually, if we want to live in power and in fellowship with the Lord, we are going to have to spend the time with God that it takes to know Him. We will need to make a deliberate effort to keep God's Word foremost in our hearts and minds. If we don't, our affections will begin to pull away from God. A consistent daily study of the scriptures is one of the most powerful ways the Lord talks to us. He focuses our need and then answers through the passage we study. It's so easy to stop building and become a maintenance man. Just maintaining what we already know but not acting on those truths. Don't let that happen to you. A mind alive to new truths to us in His Word results in a heart ablaze with new excitement for the Lord. Dullness is on the way out when there is no area where we resist His intervention.

(2) BY PRAYING.

Anyone who feels dullness creeping in must ask: Has my prayer life become a bore? It is hard carrying on a conversation when you feel no-one is listening. It's different again when you know that you are getting through. Furthermore, you are in touch with someone who promises to help and has the power to come through. Only one kind of prayer does that. All other kinds lead to frustration. An air-pilot contacted the control power with a faltering voice,

"I am 300 miles from land, 600 feet high, and running out of fuel. Please instruct: Over." The tower responded, "Repeat after me, Our Father which art in heaven, hallowed be Thy name, Thy kingdom come Thy will be done...."

This story (which is almost certainly apocryphal) reminds us of something we need to hear: it is not that we say prayers as a last ditch of hope. Prayer must be for real to the God who can deliver. Jude underlines what real prayer is. It is praying in the Holy Spirit. What is that? Perhaps it will help to say what it is not. It is the opposite of praying in the flesh. Which is prayer, all by myself. It may have perfect diction, beautiful phraseology, wonderful grammar, but it is all from me. It's ditty praying, *"Lord bless me and my wife, son John and his wife, us four and no more!"*

A person may live in the Spirit but momentarily walk after the flesh (see Gal. 5:25;). In the same way a Christian may live in the Spirit but pray in the flesh. One way of doing this is to ask amiss (James 4:3;). We put wrong requests to God to gratify our own lusts.

So, what is praying in the Spirit? It is praying in the will of God. It is prayer in co-operation with the intercessory work of the Spirit. It is the only kind of praying that can rightly be called 'true prayer.' This quality of prayer is not a luxury. There is no effective prayer at all if the Spirit is absent. The Holy Spirit is there to help all those who do not know how to pray. With the Spirit there is direction and strength in your prayer. Without the Spirit we are left to ourselves, and the result is a dull saying of words to the air. The key question is: How does one pray in the Spirit? At this point I hesitate to write further. There are so many books about prayer, and yet still little true praying. I do not wish to add to the pile! However, if it means anything at all, it must mean that we must be "in the Spirit" ourselves.

You may say, surely a person who is a true believer has God's indwelling Spirit already. Yes, but that does not mean that the believer is 'in the Spirit.' There is a difference between the Spirit being in the believer, and the believer being in the Spirit. The Apostle John was in the Spirit on the Lord's day (Revelation 1:10). It was a special place. Therefore, he receives special insights from the Lord. Real prayer means that we must prepare ourselves. Shut out the world, be calm and quiet before the Lord. Jesus said, "If you remain in me and my words remain in you, ask whatever you wish, and it will be given you" (John 15:7).

Our desires will be transformed as we remain in His presence. Remind yourself of the one way of access to the Father, Jesus Christ and Him crucified. "Let us then approach the throne of grace with confidence, so that we may receive mercy and find grace to help us in our time of need." (Hebrews 4:16) If your heart is not warmed by thinking of this means of access, you are not praying in the Spirit. That in turn leads to a realisation of God's presence. In prayer, try to picture our Lord praying for that person. Listen to the intercession. You will learn things you never knew and gain insight on co-operating with the Spirit as you pray. Robert McCheyne testified to this form of prayer. "If I could hear Christ praying for me in the next room, I would not fear a million enemies. Yet distance makes no difference. He is praying for me."

Try that in prayer. It will fill you with confidence about your personal needs. Then do the same thing for other people. As Romans 8:26; says, "We do not know what we ought to pray, but the Spirit intercedes for us with groans that words cannot express." Our Lord can pray for our need, and instruct us how to pray for others! The exciting thing is that then we can pray with new assurance because we know how to pray.

(3) BY KEEPING.

The third requirement to avoid dullness is that we keep ourselves in the love of God. At first glance these words might seem to contradict Jude's opening assertion that we are "kept by Jesus Christ" (Jude 1:1). This is not the case. Jude does not say, "keep on loving God," but directs us to enjoy God's love in all its reality. God never stops loving us, but we can stop enjoying that love. Any relationship where you can close yourself off from another will become bland. Jude tells us how to keep ourselves in the love of God. It is by appreciating the mercy of the Lord. To become a Christian you must recognise you had no worth with God by which you could achieve God's acceptance.

Discovering Great Secrets

You have one hope alone - God's mercy. We are all looking for a sense of worth. What people strive all their lives to achieve is handed to us right at the beginning when we believe in Jesus Christ. According to the gospel, we can receive it but we cannot earn it. That is good news. No wonder the Apostle Paul wrote to Timothy, "I obtained mercy." Paul never got over the wonder of it all. The experience of God's love, and the joy in the relationship comes when we know that God has really accepted us. This can only be enjoyed by affirming God's mercy. God's mercy is the expression of His love towards us. It is very important to realise that justice and mercy are not alternatives. You do not choose between them. If you choose mercy you show at first justice, and then go beyond. God will give everybody what they deserve. At first He will be just to all people, but with some He will go beyond - this is mercy. We experience mercy now through faith in Jesus Christ. Yet Jude says, "I have to wait for the mercy of God. I do not possess all that God has to give me of mercy." You can look back and say, "Great are His mercies." You can look at today and say, "His mercies are new every day" (Lamentations 3:22;). You can look forward and say, "His mercy is to be extended." We keep ourselves in the love of God by realising we never outgrow a need of God's mercy. If we cease to be amazed at the mercy God extends to us, our love for Him grows cold, the relationship formal. Dullness is on the way. The question all this brings into sharp focus is this: On what basis does God give His mercy? The answer is marvellous.

First of all, God chooses to give mercy to those who ask Him for it. Jesus makes that clear in His parable of the Pharisee and the Tax Collector (Luke 18:9 - 14). The shattering truth is we don't ask for mercy. We don't think we need it. How often do we hear people begging for mercy in our church prayer meetings? We pray for health, family needs, a marriage problem, and much beside. How often do we ask to receive mercy? We may say it from a book in a church service. I am not referring to the formal reciting of words. How often do we ask for mercy in the privacy of our bedroom?

Discovering Great Secrets

Does that mean that we have to confess that we are sinners? Don't we ever outgrow that state of contrition? Even if we admit that we are sinners in need of mercy, aren't we saved by grace? Isn't that what Christianity is all about? Must we hit bottom again and again to be able to know God? Aren't there things we can do to clean up our act so that we have something to show God as the fruit of our lives?

We misunderstand sin. It is not only separation from God, but also from our purpose, and potential. We never outgrow our need for God's love, acceptance, help and strength. As I write this I am conscious of areas of my life and relationship where I need God desperately. My opportunities, not just my failures, push me back to Him constantly. Assurance of His mercy initiates aspirations to continue to grow. God is not finished with us. Therefore we are never finished.

Right at this moment, are you conscious of things said or unsaid, done or left undone, that jab at your conscience? Who can live any day without a sense of opportunities missed as well as overt sins that have hurt ourselves and others?

Paul calls himself the "chief of sinners" at a time when he was a leading communicator of the gospel (1 Timothy 1:15). The closer he got to the Lord, the greater was his need for Him. When I used the word "mercy", I seem to get God's ear. I seem to touch His heart. Can you remember when you last asked God for His mercy? Obtaining mercy issues in certain blessings. This is why the writer to the Hebrews said, "Let us then approach the throne of grace with confidence, so that we may receive mercy and find grace to help us in our time of need." Mercy issues in the blessing of forgiveness and guidance.

Ask for God's mercy. That leads to the second thing we discover as the basis for receiving mercy. It is the result of communicating it to other people. "Blessed are the merciful for they will be shown mercy," said Jesus (Matt. 5:7). Mercy is like electricity, it must have two contact points before it can flow. It can't flow into your heart unless it can flow out of your heart.

It's not that we show mercy just to get mercy; that's not it. We don't give to get. That's not the spirit of mercy, but it does happen that the merciful become the obvious recipients of mercy. The merciful see what sin has done in people's lives and rather than shunning them, they provide mercy. Haven't you reached out at times and discovered that not only did you give, but God gave to you?

Will you join me in saying . . .
"Lord, I have received of your mercy.
Help me now to be a channel through whom your mercy can flow."

Do you know someone who is lonely?
Do you know someone who is sick?
Do you know someone who is hurting through a death or divorce?
If the Spirit of God assigns it, won't you reach out in mercy? Dull Christians are usually not involved in deep, supportive relationships. Anyone who feels dullness creeping in must ask certain questions:
"Have I kept myself in the love of God by asking the Lord for his mercy? Am I open to listen and be the kind of friend others can trust implicitly because I communicate mercy?"

If life is not exciting, if you don't feel a sense of adventure, then you are living in the ruts of dullness. This could be the last day of dullness for you. Discover the joy of an intimate relationship with Christ. Build your faith, pray in the Spirit, keep in God's love - and I can assure you that life will not be 'dull'. You will experience our Lord Jesus Christ bringing you eternal life. Knowing Jesus Christ is eternal life. They are reciprocal (John 17:3;). The Greek language has two words to express the idea of life. Jude uses "zoe" rather than "bios" (verse 21). The latter refers to the duration of life and to what sustains it. Jude uses the former word which indicates all that is the highest in life.

Discovering Great Secrets

Discovering Great Secrets

Chapter 10
I KNOW WHERE I'M GOING
To Him Who Is Able

A sixteen year old bought a bulletin board and wrote notes to remind herself of duties and dates. One day her mother read the routine messages: "Clean room. Mend skirt. Baby-sit Saturday." Mother smiled when she read, "Assume new personality." At least that's a beginning. This teenager was wanting to do it! But it's not as easy as all that.

If you could change something about your personality, what would it be? Many people long for a greater confidence about their lives. Our confident exteriors can be misleading. Inside may be a very insecure person.

As we study Jude's epistle, we can consider what it means to become a God-confident person. This is something far better than the poor substitute of self-confidence. Jude is not simply trying to round off the epistle in an inspiring way. Jude has just made reference to doubters and stragglers. Now he would have us know that we can live with confidence.

CONFIDENCE... WHAT DO YOU MEAN?

The word "confidence" from the Latin root means "thorough, altogether faith." Confidence is altogether faith. Confidence is associated to dependability. We don't spend our every waking moment feeling insecure about gravity. Experience satisfies us that when we swing our legs out of bed in the morning they will hit the floor not the ceiling! None of us would be tempted to revive our confidence in gravity by leaping off a high building! Confidence however in other people and ourselves is a different matter. People are neither reliable nor always to be relied upon.

A popular answer to this problem is to try to build self-confidence. Positive-thinking teaching often falls into this trap. Emile Coue taught a principle at the turn of the century that has caught on. Twenty times, twice each day say out loud, "Every day in every way, I am getting better and better." He claimed it would help exploit your full potential. New Age thinking is one development of this, with its 'buzz' words of 'the Higher Self', 'personal growth' and 'enlightened fulfilment' in its vocabulary.

Of course there is some truth in 'positive thinking' teaching. The image you have of yourself today exists because of the experiences of the past. Those experiences have not made you the way you are, they do mould you to believe you are the way you are. Believing you can become a different kind of person can be very releasing. On the other hand, I am reminded of the little ditty, "He tackled the thing that couldn't be done, with a will he went right to it. He tackled the thing that couldn't be done, and found he couldn't do it!" The problem with self-confidence is that the self is not reliable.

Now we are at the crux of the matter. We all fail too often to be worthy of 'altogether faith.' We crash when a difficulty comes. We are unable to cope when confronted with the needs of people. The stress of life steals our peace of mind. We battle against disappointments. We don't measure up to life's demands. We need confidence in regard to prayer, so as to obtain our petitions. We need confidence as Christians to make the glory of Jesus known to other people. But we feel so impotent and incapable.

The reason is that we were never meant to be self-confident. We were created for a relationship with Jesus Christ. He alone can give us a genuine, lasting confidence for daily living. His ability can be the buttress for our inability. What he has done, and is ready to do for us again can bring to us the confidence of an 'altogether faith.'

Discovering Great Secrets

(1) GOD'S ABILITY

That's the confidence-building affirmation of Jude's "To him who is able!" pledge. Allow your mind to go round and round this truth until it grips you. Let it do you good. This is possibly an echo from the Psalms where the Psalmist describes the disasters from which God preserves him in terms of his feet stumbling or slipping (Psalm 38:16; 56:13; 66:9; 73:2; 91:12; 116:8; 121:3).

Three times in the New Testament praise is given to the God Who is able. In Romans 16:25; Paul gives praise to the God Who is able to establish us. God is the One Who can give us a foundation for life which nothing and no one can ever shake. In Ephesians 3:20; Paul gives praise to God Who is able to do far more than we can ever ask or even dream of. God is the God whose grace no man has ever exhausted, and on Whom no claim can ever be too much. Jude offers his praise to the God Who is able. We must keep ourselves in God's love in verse 21. The word used there is *terein* meaning 'watch'. Here *phulassein* is used meaning 'guard'. We watch we stay close to the Lord, but only He can guard us so that we do not fall.

True confidence is built on the assurance that our Lord knows what we need, provides for us according to His perfect timing, and intervenes to help us. Christ-confidence replaces self-confidence when we realise He is able when we are unable. We need power and wisdom. Christ is the power of God and the wisdom of God (1 Corinthians 1:24;). Look to Him, and ask, in what way can He meet the needs which exist in our daily experience? We are to manifest the life given to us by Christ Who is able to protect us.

Meeting our need.
But how can we meet our need? It is not by feeling, or yearning, or crying, that this confidence can ever be ours. The answer is, "Christ is your life" (Colossians 3:3;); 'Christ is all, and in all' (Colossians 3:11). Then I have nothing to do but let Christ Himself exert upon me the power which He bestowed

103

upon me. He takes my personality, and uses it, and it is to Him that I look - not to it - to make His ability known in the person which He has deigned to inhabit.

Paul in his prayer for the Ephesian Church can say, "I pray that out of his glorious riches he may strengthen you with power through his Spirit in your inner being, so that Christ may dwell in your hearts through faith. And I pray that you, being rooted and established in love may have power, together with all the saints, to grasp how wide and long and high and deep is the love of Christ" (Eph. 3:16-18;). It is the power that is in Christ which passes into the believer, and takes possession of His own, when the believer is made willing.

Don't try to psyche yourself up to believe He is able. "If anyone is in Christ, he is a new creation; the old has gone, the new has come!" (2 Corinthians 5:17). What is this newness? It is the life of Christ, and that life of Christ being put into you, your intellect and emotions do not need to be stirred by trying to feel it. Take calmly what God offers. I am Christ's because He died for me. Christ is mine because He is given to me. Because He gave Himself for me He can now give Himself to me. Whatever God requires of me I am enabled for, if only He is trusted as He should be.

How shall we say then, "I can't live the life of Christ; others may have the ability, but it is impossible for me to do so"?

Will you see that the power of Christ does rest on me when I acknowledge my own lack of strength absolutely, and take what He is pleased to give - Himself. As I take Him I take power and wisdom. Therefore, I can be confident there never can be a mistake as to the pathway in which I should walk, there never can be a mistake as to the direction given to me. Even more amazing, there never can be failure in regard to the supply, because 'power' with all the activities of 'wisdom', passes into my being according to its need. So, with regard to this life that is to be lived, it is "I no longer live, but Christ lives in me" (Galatians 2:20), consequently there must be the supply of every need of my nature.

Again, we lack confidence with God in prayer. We say, "I long to pray better, I long for the power of prayer!" You forget that "The Spirit himself *intercedes for us with groans that words cannot express" (Romans 8:26;). In the best of prayers it is not I that speak, but Christ that speaks in me. So that when we go before God the Father to plead for blessing of any kind whatever, for ourselves or others, it is Christ who takes the need expressed by us, through the Holy Spirit, and places it before God the Father in heaven. It must be answered, because "My Father will give you anything you ask in my name,"* said Jesus (John 16:23).

Or you come, perhaps, under the pressure of temptation. You come with your temptation and say, "I just can't resist!" No, but look at 2 Corinthians 9:8; God is able to make all grace abound to you, so that in all things at all times, having all that you need, you will abound in every good work." Is there any excuse for that sin which you are cowering under, despising, and yet saying, "It has power that I can't overcome!"? No, you cannot, but God can.

BUT GOD

Have you noticed the 'buts' in the Bible? The 'buts' of man are always for misgiving and apprehension. We say, "I'm feeling fine today, but . . ." "I've got money in my pocket today, but . . ."

We invariably mean that things will be bad tomorrow. Everywhere in the Bible you find that the 'buts' of God are always for good. Focus on the thought. Instead of coming with your excuses for weakness to cope, just acknowledge "I am unable to change, but Jesus Christ is my 'all in all.'" Then go out to live a life that will exhibit Christ and not self, a life that is full of power with God in prayer, and is able to resist temptation at all points. Christ confident people have a boldness in living.

Discovering Great Secrets

The question now must be put, "How can this be? In what way shall it be applied to every area of life, and make me without excuse if I continue in sin?" The answer is in John 15:5, "Apart from me you can do nothing." That word of the Lord Jesus is not our ordinary English word 'apart'. Someone may say, "Without an umbrella I can't keep off the rain." Though the umbrella is a separate thing from himself, yet by its use he can keep off the rain. However, the Greek word for 'apart' implies 'separate from' him we can do nothing. It implies that we must be connected with Christ in such a way that He is one with us and we with Him, so that there is nothing commanded by God for which we are not enabled. This is why Paul could say with supreme confidence, "I can do everything through Him who gives me strength" (Philippians4:13).

Jabez Bunting was a Methodist preacher of last century. One Sunday, he gave out his text - Philippians 4:13, 'I can do all things.' Then he dropped the Bible on the desk and said, "Paul, thou art a liar! 'I can do all things.' Paul, thou art a fearful liar! 'I can do all things.' Paul, thou art a shameful liar! 'I can do all things *through Christ which strengthened Me*.' Oh Paul, I beg your pardon. That is quite another thing, Paul; you are not a liar at all."

The boldness of Paul was not rooted in self-confidence, but in Christ. Christ's message had unlocked the truth. Christ's death was an assurance of his salvation. Christ's resurrection was a final validation of the ultimate power of God. Christ's presence in Paul as indwelling Lord was the motive power to try anything He guided. Eight times, in Philippians 4 (verses 1, 2, 4, 7, 10, 13, 19, 21), Paul brings in the words 'in Christ' or 'in the Lord.' Again and again his whole being revelled in the habitation which God had taken up in him. He was consolidated into Christ. The basic conviction which undergirds true confidence is "And my God will meet all your needs according to his glorious riches in Christ Jesus" (Philippians 4:19;). The more we know Christ, the more confident we become. The possibility of His power becomes a reality.

Discovering Great Secrets

Lack of self-confidence is a blessing if it leads us to Christ confidence. He is available, but let me ask you a straight question. When did you last pray to God for real spiritual growth in power, in love and usefulness? Start praying and praying and praying, that you may be strengthened with the Lord's power more and more. There is no place we can go where He will not be with us; no problem we can face for which His power will be inadequate; no person we will deal with in whom He has not been working; no situation where He has not preceded us and will show the way. If we ask Him to come through us into each situation and trust Him to do so, He will. The Lord living His life in us and through us will be glorious. I can expect anything, hope for everything, and fear nothing. Like Paul we can say, "I am confident in the Lord" (Galatians 5:10). So Jude's assurance can be yours, *"To him who is able."* Lord again. We begin to hate the things we once loved and find ourselves actually not sinning. The joy derived from this is marvellous.

We need to see that God is able at every level of life. He can solve our problem of giving up rather than going on if by conviction we know that "our God is able to keep."

Are you, worried about something? The tragedy of the load of worry is that it is an unnecessary burden. That sounds a shallow saying, and everyone knows how difficult it is to avoid, but I will say it, nevertheless. Our God "is able to do immeasurably more than all we ask or imagine, according to his power that is at work within us" (Ephesians 3:20;). The word 'immeasurably' is the Greek word perisseou, and that means 'overflowing' like a glass of water full to the brim and running over. Paul isn't content, he puts in front huperekperissou, giving the picture of the whole thing going over the top like the Victoria Falls! That is the promise of God. What are you worried about, with a God like this?

Are you worried about your salvation? "He is able to guard what I have entrusted to him for that day" (2 Timothy 1:12). This is our God, *"Able to keep us from falling."*

Discovering Great Secrets

(2) GOD'S ACCEPTANCE.

We may sin or be deceived and lose the joy of our salvation or the blessings that God wants to give us, but God is persistent in pulling us back to Himself. It is His desire for us to be presented "before his glorious throne without fault and with great joy." Not only do we have God's power to keep us, but there is coming a day in which we will be able to stand still without cowering in His presence. Not merely guiltless. We have been regarded as guiltless for a long time by virtue of Christ having satisfied divine justice. We are not being presented guiltless, we are that already. We will be presented morally and physically perfect. How can God do that? The only explanation is, by changing us into the likeness of Christ. Jesus claimed to gaze into the face of the Father. Some day we shall be like Him, and see God and live forever. No more will we feel a temptation to selfishness, lust, egoism or resentment. The power of God will transform our minds and wills. Our bodies will also be changed. A small child said to her friend, "I wonder how old Joanne is? The little boy replied, "I don't know, but I bet she won't see four again." We do get old, but think of it - our bodies that are now frail, given an eternal healing.

No wonder Jude says that this will be accompanied with "great joy." Is that the joy we feel or the joy of Christ has in presenting us? It is probably the joy God Himself experiences. Our joy is the consequence of seeing His joy and what follows. What a motive to persist to the end.

(3) GOD'S ATTRIBUTES.

Essentially, I believe life's biggest questions are the result of the fact that our God has been too small, our vision of Him too limited. The reason some people struggle is that they have the wrong idea about God. Most of the struggles we endure are the result of a profound misunderstanding of God's real nature and of what he is ready and willing to do in our lives. The main thing that Jude would have us see now is that God is to be trusted and is worthy of our obedience. He is "the only

Discovering Great Secrets

God our Saviour," says Jude. You only need one when he is like our God.

"God writes with a pen that never blots,
speaks with a tongue that never skips,
and acts with a hand that never fails." (Anon.)

Human language cannot comprehend the meaning of the four words used by Jude to ascribe praise to God. What are glory, majesty, power and authority? The word 'glory' more than any other in the Bible defies definition. "Glory is doctrine gone emotional!" says Calvin Miller. Perhaps the best that we can say is that it is the great reality of God, the displayed supremacy of God. You've said it all by using the word 'glory', because the glory of God is the sum total of all God's attributes. However, Jude wants to say three more things. To Him be "majesty." This word simply means 'greatness.' God tolerates royalty using the title. A day is coming when it will be attributed to God alone. We don't need to wait. We can crown Him as great now. "The fixed point in the universe, the unalterable fact, is the throne of God" (G. Campbell Morgan). Men today want 'power.' A day is coming when God will demonstrate His supremacy and superiority. Affirm this power now by humbling yourself under His hand (Luke 14:11).

Jude needed one more word, for after all, the devil was given the power of death (Hebrews 2:14). Thank God He has "authority." It means the freedom to do whatever He desires without hindrance. The power given to the devil is eclipsed by the greater power and authority that God has Himself. There is a day coming when through Jesus Christ our Lord, all injustice will end. These attributes have always belonged to God, do now, and will for ever more. All Jude can do is say, "Amen."

Let the words of Peter Marshall become your motto: "It is better to fail in a cause that will ultimately succeed than to succeed in a cause that will ultimately fail." Jesus Christ, the hope of the world, is alive. He has conquered death! He goes before us to show the way!

There is no place where we can go where He has not been before us; there is no one with whom we must deal whom Christ has not prepared for us; there is no situation in which we are to live where He had not preceded us; there is no temptation, trial, or tragedy in which He has not entered before us; there is no joy we are to know which He has not made ready beforehand. We can keep going when we have a Lord like this.

When our trust is no longer based on human adequacy or ability or perfection, we can place our trust in the Lord and face whatever life has to offer. Christ has won and will win. Be sure of that! Say it to your soul and then live it, through Jesus Christ your Lord.

We can - and why not?

Discovering Great Secrets

Chapter 11
ENCOURAGING WORDS FOR JOURNEY'S END
The Dead At Christ's Coming

In 1996, Jeanne Calment was the oldest living human whose age could be verified. On her 120th birthday, she was asked to describe her vision for the future. "Very brief," she said. Another woman was asked the benefits of living to the age of 102. After a pause, she answered, "No peer pressure!"

The apostle Paul has something to say about death we all need to know. I guarantee it can encourage you. "Brothers, we do not want you to be ignorant about those who fall asleep, or to grieve like the rest of men, who have no hope. We believe that Jesus died and rose again and so we believe that God will bring with Jesus those who have fallen asleep in him. According to the Lord's own word, we tell you that we who are still alive, who are left till the coming of the Lord will certainly not precede those who have fallen asleep. For the Lord himself will come down from heaven, with a loud command, with the voice of the archangel and with the trumpet call of God and the dead in Christ will rise first. After that, we who are still alive and are left will be caught up together with them in the clouds to meet the Lord in the air. And so we will be with the Lord forever. Therefore encourage each other with these words." (1 Thessalonians 4:13-18)

The next major world event is the return of the Lord Jesus Christ. There are 1,845 references in the Old Testament alone and a total of 17 books that give it eminence. Of the 260 chapters in the whole New Testament, there are 318 references to Christ's Second Coming. That averages one out of every 30 verses. Furthermore, 23 of the 27 New Testament books refer to the Second Coming. Interestingly, three of these four books are single chapter letters, which were written to specific persons on a single subject. Another interesting factor is that for every prophecy on the first coming of Christ – when He was born as a baby in Bethlehem – there are eight prophecies on Christ's Second Coming.

You cannot really preach the Gospel adequately and ignore this subject. True, the Gospel centres on the cross. There are approximately 300 references to it in scripture. No other event has as many references as the cross and the Second Coming of Christ. Our faith looks back to the cross. Our hope looks forward to His coming. We should live in love right in the middle of these great events. I shall not answer all your questions in this chapter. However, we can discuss some fascinating, comforting and challenging information.

Paul preached the whole Gospel to the Thessalonians. He did not want them ignorant about the future hope of the believer. So excited was Paul that this might happen in his lifetime, he managed to convey that awesome fact. Of course every generation of Christians hope that they will not pass through the process of physical death. We are looking for the up-taker not the undertaker. This was now troubling some believers. They were expecting the Lord to return any day. They felt their loved ones who had died would not be resurrected until the final resurrection at the end of time. They would not see them again until that far-off event. Death leaves the impression that the one who has died is out of things. This was worrying the Thessalonians. It was a natural reaction.

Paul wrote to dispel their ignorance. They are going to get front seats. They will not miss anything. "God will bring with Jesus those who have fallen asleep in him" (1 Thess. 4:14). That takes all the fear away. It will be lovely to go straight to Jesus. It will be marvellous not to have to go through the process of death. A Christian can be torn two ways. Like Paul we may say, "I am torn between two: I desire to depart and be with Christ, which is better by far; but it is more necessary for you that I remain in the body" (Phil. 1:23, 24). Often it is more necessary for us! There is still much that God must do in us and through us before we say our final good night to the world. If you could see a single Christian in glory you would not want to pull them back into this world. You would envy their position. If you have blessing here, that is nothing to the benefit of eternity. Therefore, the Christian is not allowed the luxury of worldly grief. We are not. "To grieve like the rest of men who have no hope" (1 Thess. 4:13).

How miserable the world is about death. A caption on a poster read: "The first two minutes of a man's life are the most critical." Graffiti underneath exclaimed: "The last two are pretty dicey as well." I doubt that there has been a culture that has spent more money on death or less time and attention to what comes after death.

The story has been told of a man who regularly read the Times Newspaper obituary column and read his own obituary. He phoned the editor, "I have just read my own obituary in your newspaper," he complained. There was a silence before the editor enquired, "Where are you speaking from now?"

The most certain fact of life is death. You can tell a Christian funeral: there may be tears, that is natural - but you know this is not the end. For the Christian it is just an address change. The fact of death is unmentionable in some company because we live in a world without God and without hope. True, we do feel the parting. Death hurts a believer.

Steve Brown writes, "I was speaking at a religious emphasis week at a Christian college. Shortly before I went to speak at the college, a woman I had known for a number of years died. She had been one of Christ's most faithful servants. Her witness had literally touched thousands of people in some exciting and positive ways. Her daughter was a student at the college and one evening after the meeting I noticed her standing in line waiting to speak to me. I was interested in what she was going to say. When she got up to me, she said, 'Mr Brown, I'm Sara Clark (not her name).' 'Sara,' I said, 'I knew your mother and I loved her. She was an inspiration to so many of us. I know this must be a difficult time for you.' 'Not at all', she said smiling. 'I know where my mother is. She is in heaven and her funeral was a witness to how our family is praising God, We saw a number of people come to know Christ at the funeral. Don't waste any pity on me, I'm a Christian.'

With uncharacteristic bluntness (well, maybe a little characteristic), I said, 'Sara don't give me that kind of balderdash. If your mother's dead and you're happy about that, you're not playing with a full deck.' Do you know what happened? She fell apart. The tears flowed for the first time in weeks. Sara and I spent a lot of time together that week talking about her mother, how she loved her and how much she missed her. Most of the time I just let her talk and cry and be angry. She had found someone who allowed her not to be 'Christian' for a change, someone who didn't reject her honest feelings. Sara is doing fine now. She still misses her mother. She knows that her mother is with Christ and Sara has a much stronger witness to her friends now because it is honest and free.

The point? Sara had been given a set of standards that as a Christian she felt she must maintain. One of those standards was that Christians praise God all the time and never deal with tragedy honestly lest they hurt their witness for Christ. By allowing people to be human, we give them permission to be free." *(When Being Good Isn't Good Enough, Stephen Brown, Crossway Books 1991).*

We feel and we grieve. But we mourn over our own loss. "I'm sorry that you have lost your wife," said a friend to a new widower. "I haven't lost her," he replied, "I know exactly where she is."

Paul dispels ignorance concerning the dead at Christ's coming. For death Paul used the phrase: "those who have fallen asleep" (v.13). That reminds me of the Children's Church Teacher who asked her class why it is important to be quiet in church. One bright little girl replied, "Because people are sleeping!" That is not what Paul had in mind, of course. The phrase "fallen asleep" is used to describe believers who have died. The term is never used in the New Testament of anyone but believers. It never says of a non-believer when he died that he "fell asleep". There is a wonderful lesson in that. It shows that death, for the believer, is nothing more than sleep.

When referring to Lazarus who had died, Jesus said, "Our friend Lazarus has fallen asleep; but I am going there to wake him up" (John 11:11). By the way, this word in Greek is where we get our word "cemetery." It was the early Christians' optimistic name for a graveyard because they knew it was a sleeping place, a dormitory for dead people who will one day be resurrected;

Have you ever wondered what it feels like to die? You practise it every night. When you fall asleep you are quietly resting. You expect to wake up again in the same room. One day it will be a place prepared by Jesus (John 14: 2, 3).

Some people have wrongly taken the apostle's phrase to mean the dead remain in an unconscious state until Jesus returns. I cannot believe that a man so alive as Paul would consider death gain if it was less than the conscious presence of Christ he experienced on earth (Phil. 1:21).

The thing we must remember in dealing with this matter of life beyond death is that when time ends, eternity begins. The Thessalonians, like us today, were projecting the sequence of time into eternity. We all wrestle with the concept of eternity. We tend to think of it as time going on limitlessly; that, as is the case here on earth, we must wait for certain events which are yet future. That is how it will be in heaven we feel, despite the fact that the Word of God seeks to show that time and eternity are two different things.

Dr. Arthur Custance, a Canadian scientist makes a helpful comment on this: "The really important thing to notice is that Time stands in the same relation to Eternity in one sense, as a large number does to infinity. There is one sense in which infinity includes a very large number, yet it is quite fundamentally different and independent of it. By analogy, reduction of Time until it gets smaller and smaller is still not Eternity. Nor do we reach Eternity by an extension of Time to great length. There is no direct pathway between Time and Eternity. They are different categories of experience." *(Doorway Paper No. 37, Arthur Custance. Published by the author).*

Augustine understood this. He devoted Book 11 of The Confessions to a discussion of time. He wrote, "What then is time? If no one asks me, I know; if I want to explain it to someone who does ask me, I do not know." When asked, "What was God doing before creation?" he states, "Since God invented time along with the created world, such a question is nonsense and merely betrays the time-bound perspective of the questioner. Before time there is only eternity and eternity of God is never ending present."

Time has sequences: past, present and future. But eternity has only one dimension: it is present, now. We struggle with that, as the Thessalonians also did.

In time I am at a desk writing these words. In a few days' time I will be back at the Good News Broadcasting recording studio to prepare some radio programmes. It will not be long before I fly abroad for some preaching engagements. That will be true only of my body. That says nothing about where my mind may be. Minds are not limited to space, or time, or sequence. They can go anywhere and experience anything at any time. Eternity is much more like that. That is why we have great difficulty understanding prophetic passages in scripture in terms of time when they are really eternal events. In eternity there is no past nor future, only the present now. Within that 'now' all events will happen.

There probably is sequence of experience in eternity, but it is not based on chronology; it is based upon spiritual readiness. There are scriptural passages that seem to support this. For instance, "The Lamb that was slain from the creation of the world" *(Rev. 13:8).* The cross happened at a particular moment

Discovering Great Secrets

in world history; we can date it. We know when the Lord Jesus Christ was slain as the Lamb of God. Yet scripture says it occurred from the creation of the world. How can you explain how this historical event took place at a certain time on earth, but is said to have occurred before the earth was properly functioning? If you try to project all the thoughts and relationships of time into eternity, you are sure to have real difficulty with this. But if you remember that in eternity all things are present at one time, then of course it is no problem.

Take another example. Paul states, "Praise be to the God and Father of our Lord Jesus Christ, who has blessed us in the heavenly realms with every blessing in Christ. For he chose us in him before the creation of the world" *(Eph. 1:3, 4).* How do you explain that? Only when you see eternity not as a series of events in a sequence of time, but as relating to us in a different way, can you explain it.

When a believer steps out of time, he is in eternity. The big event of the future is that Jesus is coming again for the believer. Surely it is this event which welcomes every believer the moment he dies. It may be many years before it happened in time. However, this person is no longer in time but eternity. The experience of that believer does not leave anyone behind. All his loved ones who know Christ are there as well. This includes his Christian descendants who were not born when he died! Since there is no past or future in heaven, this must surely be true. Even those who, in time, stand beside a grave and weep and then go home to an empty house, are in his experience, with him in heaven.

Dr. Custance reasons further, "The experience of each saint is shared by all other saints, by those who have preceded and those who are to follow. For them all, all history, all intervening time between death and the Lord's return is suddenly annihilated so that each one finds to his amazement that Adam, too, is just dying and joining him on his way to meet the Lord: and Abraham and David, Isaiah and the Beloved John, Paul and Augustine, Hudson Taylor and you and I – all in one

Discovering Great Secrets

wonderful experience meeting the Lord in a single instant together, without precedence and without the slightest consciousness of delay, none being late and none too early."
(Dr. Custance, Doorway Paper No. 37 Published by the author).

I am aware of a problem passage in this connection in Revelation 6: 9-11. John is shown a scene of "The souls of those who had been slain because of the word of God and the testimony they had maintained. They call out in a loud voice, 'How long, Sovereign Lord, holy and true, until you judge the inhabitants of the earth and avenge our blood?' Then each of them was given a white robe and they were told to wait a little longer, until the number of their fellow-servants and brothers who were to be killed as they had been was completed." Does this contradict what I have written? Here are souls in heaven needing to wait for God to avenge them. What is the explanation? I think that this is best understood by the fact that these martyred believers are empathising with the conditions of earth. They are in eternity. They have moved into eternal relationships, but they are concerned about what is happening on earth. On earth there is always the awareness of time, delay and waiting. Since John is still on earth (on the island of Patmos) their expression of concern must be voiced in the language of time.

I believe that Paul knew the difference between time and eternity, but he reassures the Thessalonians, without becoming academic, that the living and the dead will be together when our Lord returns. That is the point at issue. He says, in effect, "Yes, you will see your loved ones immediately when the Lord returns. Whether you join that event when you die or whether the Lord comes while you are yet alive your loved ones will be with Him." That is the focus of his thoughts.

Since writing the above lines I have returned from Sweden. I am heading home, which is not far from where John and Charles Wesley had their childhood. It reminds me that many of our great hymns were produced to help the believers die well.

Discovering Great Secrets

Charles Wesley's splendid words: *"Happy if with my latest breath*
I may gasp his name preach him to all and cry in death:
Behold! Behold, the Lamb"*.

You cannot have a more admirable ambition than to die well. Christianity not only teaches you how to live but how to die. If you are in Jesus what happened to Jesus will happen to you. When He died He committed His spirit to the Father and He rose again. We will all be together, do not be concerned about that. You will find your loved ones again when the Lord returns.

How will it happen?
You will get confused if you regard the coming of the Lord as though it were a single event, an immediate and once-for-all appearing. The coming of the Lord is a series of events. This series has a dramatic beginning, as Paul describes here, with Jesus coming to take His living and dead believers to be with Him. It has an even more dramatic ending when as Jesus Himself said, He would materialise Himself to the entire world: "He is coming with the clouds and every eye will see him" *(Rev. 1:7)*. That is a different event from the one here described. You cannot make those fit together. In between them is a period of time during which Jesus is present on the earth though not always visibly so.

When Scripture talks about the coming, (Greek word, *parousia*) it sometimes looks at the beginning of that series, sometimes it looks at the end of it or in-between. The *parousia* of Jesus is a series of events. His first coming lasted around 30 years and included a variety of events. After our Lord's resurrection for 40 days Jesus was here on earth. He appeared to the disciples in Jerusalem and in Galilee. People heard reports that He was around but nobody could find Him except when He chose to be seen. That is the same condition that will prevail on earth during this time of the coming of the Lord. If we comprehend that, it will help us greatly to grasp what is described.

Discovering Great Secrets

There are three sounds connected with this initial appearing of Jesus. These sounds affect different groups.

First: the command of the Lord. "The Lord himself will come down from heaven with a loud command" (v.16). This is a military term that was issued when the troops were "at ease" and it was time for them to "fall in". Who is that cry addressed to? Jesus Himself said, "A time is coming and has now come when the dead will hear the voice of the Son of God and those who hear will live" (John 5:25). When Jesus stood before the tomb of Lazarus, He: "called in a loud voice, 'Lazarus come out!'" (John 11.43). To the amazement of the crowd the dead man appeared at the doorway of the tomb. As many commentators have pointed out, if Jesus had not said "Lazarus", He would have emptied the graveyard! Someone once described Jesus as "The world's worst funeral director – he broke up every funeral he ever attended, including his own" *(Dennis Bennett, Nine O'clock in the Morning, Kingsway)*. But the hour is coming when all the dead shall hear the voice of the Son of God and come out! That is what Paul is talking about here. Stanley Spencer has painted a churchyard scene with bodies coming out of their tombs. Some think it grim. Those with eyes to see are excited. The cry of command is addressed to the dead; to those in the tombs who had "fallen asleep in him" (v.14).

The second sound is the voice of the Archangel. The only angel in the Bible called an archangel is Michael. Though Gabriel is a great angel he is not called an archangel in the Scripture. Michael has a special responsibility towards Israel. An angel said to Daniel, "At that time Michael, the great prince who protects your people, will arise" (Dan. 12:1). "Your people" means Israel. Michael is always connected with Israel. Michael will arise and then there shall be a resurrection. As Jesus comes down with His booming command, Michael's voice is echoing behind him. Those who are in the tombs will come out (Dan. 12:2). Also, the living nation of Israel will be summoned to a new relationship with God. Details of this event concern the 144,000 Israelites, twelve tribes of Israel (see Rev. 7 and

14). These will be called into a fresh relationship with Jesus to follow Him wherever He goes on earth during the time of His presence. He is imperceptible to the world but visible to them. That all begins when Jesus returns for His church and the archangel calls Israel into a new relationship with the Lord.

The third sound is the trumpet call of God. The Bible is filled with references to trumpets and they have a number of different meanings. In Exodus 19 a very loud trumpet was used to call the people out to meet with God.

In Zechariah 9:14, a trumpet was used as a signal that the Lord was about to rescue His people. The trumpet sounds forth at the Rapture because God's people are called out in order to be rescued.

The world will not hear this call only those to whom it is addressed. Paul pinpoints those in 1 Corinthians 15:51, "We will not all sleep but we will all be changed – in a flash, in the twinkling of an eye, at the last trumpet." What an excellent verse for a Church Crèche, "We will not all sleep but we will all be changed!" But this verse is especially addressed to living believers. We are not all going to die, but we shall all be changed. The biggest Christian meeting ever is coming. No wonder it will be in the air. There is not a stadium on earth that could contain it. Satan is called: "the prince of the air". On that day the air will belong to the believer. This is a statement of priority. That would have calmed the concerns of the Thessalonians. Notice that it is the dead "in Christ" who are raised. This is only a resurrection of believers. The unsaved are left in their graves to be raised at the Great White Throne judgment one thousand years later (see Rev. 20:5).

What a marvellous hope we have. "Therefore encourage each other with these words" (v.18). This is the ultimate family reunion. Revel in the comfort it brings in old age as the hour of death becomes more a conscious thought.

Discovering Great Secrets

Discovering Great Secrets

Chapter 12
IT HAD TO END
A Time To Mourn

There once lived a Greek man by the name of *Hippocrates*. He was a physician who is, at least in our day, actually referred to as *"the father of medicine"*. Hippocrates' wrote in what is known as 'Precepts,' these very interesting words, "Healing is a matter of time." This could be paraphrased to read, *"Healing from pain or loss takes time."* That echoes some other wise sayings about life such as Ecclesiastes - *"There is a time to weep and a time to mourn"* (or literally, to grieve.) He also said, *"It takes time to heal."*
However, many well-meaning Christians would quote the part of 1 Thessalonians 4:13 that says, . . . *you will not grieve* . . . What does the rest of the verse say? . . . you will not grieve *as do the rest who have not hope.*

No inoculation . . .
Christians have not been inoculated against grieving by simply coming to the Cross. The experience of a Christian is not somehow going to be devoid of any suffering; any cause for mourning. In fact, the Christian experience may be absolutely the opposite.

We know this by a two word verse of scripture which tells us, *"Jesus wept"* (John 11:35). If it is spiritual not to weep or to grieve or to mourn, then we need to rewrite our spirituality. In this verse, Jesus, who is the most spiritual individual to ever walk the face of the earth, is sobbing at the grave of His friend Lazarus. He knows what he will do in a few moments time – He will raise Lazarus from the dead. I think Jesus was weeping because he knew that He could not do that immediately for every believer. That there is a gap in time and we do part – but not without hope.

Discovering Great Secrets

Little grief, big grief . . .
We all experience, what we would call, *little grief* or *big grief.* Little grief may seem large at the moment they occur, but in retrospect, perhaps not as great. However, grief is there.

GRIEF OPPORTUNITIES . . .

Relocation
Grief is incurred when moving away from one location to another. The uprooting of the network of friendships that has been established causes grief.

Retirement
A man or woman is told that they are now too old to contribute to the company. It is a point of grief.

Rejection
A person works diligently for advancement but a job is given to someone else. This is an opportunity for grief. What about the loss of being dumped by a girlfriend or boyfriend? What about a divorce you don't want, or children who walk away from you?

There's a story I heard told about a young man who was determined to win the affection of a girl who refused to even see him. He figured the way to win her was by writing letters to her. So he wrote one love letter to her every single day. This did not seem to work, so he increased his output to two and three a day. Finally, she married the postman!

We cannot live life without experiencing grief in a thousand different ways.

JOB'S EXPERIENCE . . .
"One day when Job's sons and daughters were feasting and drinking wine at the oldest brother's house, a messenger came to Job and said, `The oxen were ploughing and the donkeys were grazing nearby, and the Sabeans attacked and carried them off. They put the servants to the sword, and I am the only one who has escaped to tell you!' (Job 1:13).

Discovering Great Secrets

Grief is a young widow who must seek a means to bring up her three children alone.

Grief is the angry reaction of a man so filled with shock, uncertainty and confusion that he strikes out at the nearest person. Grief is the emptiness that comes when you eat alone after eating with another for many years. Grief is teaching yourself somehow to go to bed without saying "goodnight" to the one who has died. Grief is the helpless wishing that things were different when you know that they are not and never will be again.

Grief comes in a variety of ways. Sometimes it comes very early. Sometimes a child experiences it. John Claypool in his book *Tracks of a Fellow Struggler* says that when he was four years old he had a puppy, a fat brown and white butterball named Jiggs. One day they were out playing in the backyard, frolicking about as puppies and little boys do. He went running inside and Jiggs was right behind him, as he did so the screen door slammed on Jiggs and broke his neck. He had a convulsion and died before his eyes. Years later, he said, "I can still remember the feeling of horror and unbelief."

For many of us grief did not come in our later years; it came very early in life – when something cherished was gone and we felt deep grief.

PEOPLE HANDLE GRIEF VERY DIFFERENTLY.

Vulnerable
I remember well conducting a funeral for a baby. The funeral director carried the coffin into the church – it was the size of a shoe box. The mother was a confident person – able to hold her own in the hard-headed business world. But she went through grief in a lonely quiet fashion. She was very vulnerable for a while.

Volatile
Other people are rather volatile, and they handle grief very differently. I conducted a funeral, and after I finished, people

125

came up to the coffin sobbing and with deep hurt. I had to keep a grip on the wife of the deceased at the grave-side because she was close to throwing herself into the grave. It was consistent with her personality; she was that kind of person. She tended to be volatile and explosive. I expected her to handle grief in that way, and she did.

Tears
A common element in all forms of grief is the importance of tears. Never deny tears to anybody. If people want to cry in the face of tragedy, let them – in fact, encourage them. Many men need to almost pray that they will learn how to cry. On average, women outlive men by about seven years. Perhaps this is primarily because men don't know how to cry. Women handle pressure, pain and grief much better than men do. Trying to be "a man" is not very healthy. Tears are healing, therapeutic and necessary. If someone has been wrenched from your side, give vent to your grief. Allow yourself God's gift for healing. Tears are part of that process.

GUIDELINES . . .
The book of Job gives us some guidelines concerning the grieving process. It shows us how one man went through it. How does Job handle his grief?

(1) NUMBED SHOCK.

"Then they sat on the ground with him for seven days and seven nights. No one said a word to him, because they saw how great his suffering was" (Job 2:13).

That was the best thing the three men did: They remained silent. The minute they opened their mouths they were useless. That is often true in times of grief. People come along with all kinds of inane, useless, unfortunate, ill-timed, trite clichés. What you really need is their love, their presence, a hug, a kiss.

Discovering Great Secrets

The best thing the three men did was to sit quietly for seven days. If they had then got up and left, they would have ministered to Job. Unfortunately, they began to talk.

Job was going through the numbed and shocked period. When it first strikes you, you feel as though you are enveloped in cotton. You are numb. I have seen people who looked strong in the face of grief, but it was the strength of numbness. The full impact of their tragedy had not dawned on them yet.

Job has lost much and is simply numb. There is nothing to say, and the friends didn't say anything worth saying.

(2) UTTER DESPAIR.

"After this, Job opened his mouth and cursed the day of his birth. He said: `May the day of my birth perish, and the night it was said, 'A boy is born!' That day – may it turn to darkness; may God above not care about it; may not light shine upon it." . . . "Why did I not perish at birth, and die as I came from the womb?" . . . "What I feared has come upon me; what I dreaded has happened to me. I have no peace, no quietness; I have no rest, but only turmoil." (Job 3, selected verses)

For Job, all meaning has collapsed. Everything is foolishness. He reaches out but he feels and touches nothing. All is murky, meaningless, lonely, anxiety-ridden. Despair is everywhere.

In the early hours of a Sunday morning the door-bell was ringing. I looked out of the window and saw a Policewoman. She told me that a man had died and his wife was so distraught – would I go to see her. My wife, Pauline, and I quickly got dressed and made our way to the home. The woman was in such utter despair -- "What will I do? What will I do?" She was frantic, she was lonely. "How do I pay the bills? Where will I live? What will I do? We have depended on each other. Now what? Why did you leave me?" When you have been close to somebody and he is now gone, utter despair overwhelms you when he leaves.

Discovering Great Secrets

(3) NOSTALGIA EXCURSIONS.

Job says: "One day it was so good. God was near…and my family was here…life was good, but now…" (Job 29).

You can feel the wrenching and the tearing in Job's words. He looks back on good memories, but now he is alone. He is broken in spirit, and his nostalgic excursion is very meaningful for him but the contrast between the then and the now hurts. When people go through the period of nostalgia, when those around you talk about the one who is deceased, encourage them.

Nostalgia is helpful. Those are good memories. Those are important memories. *Claim them!* Our reactions go in two directions during such times. One aspect of nostalgia is that we begin to idealise the deceased.

One pastor was thirty-three when he died, and he was an excellent preacher and a fine pastor. He became even a *better* preacher and a *better* pastor after he died. Memory does that.

The other aspect of nostalgia is more harmful. Often *guilt* sets in, and we wonder why we didn't do more. "If only I could have known that my wife was going to pass away, we would have travelled more". "If I could have known that my husband was never going to reach retirement, we would have enjoyed a lot of things and not put them off."

(4) ANGER AND RESENTMENT.

Job speaks about God, *"He throws me into the mud, and I am reduced to dust and ashes. I cry out to you, O God, but you do not answer; I stand up, but you merely look at me. You turn on me ruthlessly; with the might of your hand you attack me. You snatch me up and drive me before the wind; you toss me about in the storm. I know you will bring me down to death, to the place appointed for all the living."* (Job 30)

Discovering Great Secrets

People in grief often become angry and resentful and feel cheated. Sometimes the anger is vented on their families. Often anger is directed against God. "God, you did it! Why did you do it?" Don't be surprised when it comes. It is part of the grieving process, and it is better to admit anger than to deny it – particularly with God.

C.S. Lewis usually wrote helpfully, with clarity and with great understanding. One of his books though, is a "downer". It is called *A Grief Observed*. In it Lewis, who married in middle age is reflecting on his own bitterness because his wife died prematurely. Across the pages of that book you can see the words, *"God, why did you do it?"*

We have human needs. God can handle them. If you feel bitterness and anger, God invites you to be yourself in His presence. We are not always sure how we will handle it, but God can handle it.

WHEN GRIEF MAKES THIS TURN - MOVE INTO A BRIGHTER LIFE.

"The Lord answered Job out of the storm. He said: "Who is this that darkens my counsel with words without knowledge? Brace yourself like a man; I will question you, and you shall answer me. Where were you when I laid the earth's foundation? Tell me, if you understand." (Job 38).

Job is given a refresher course in theology. God reminds him that arguing about justice and injustice is an inappropriate response to the working of God, because justice and injustice is what God does or does not do. Justice is what God does. That is His standard, not our perspective. God reminds Job that He made everything, and He gives everything. He says, in effect, "What right do you have, Job, to talk about the good gifts I give you? You don't deserve any of them, and I gave them to you. They were an act of grace in the first place. I am a Giver of good gifts that you didn't deserve, and just be grateful that you ever had them at all." God gives Job a whole new perspective.

Discovering Great Secrets

He says, "What I do is for your good as well." Job begins to recognise that God is on the throne and that God can handle his problems. He begins to release all the treasures he held so tightly.

Once we begin to release our treasures, God can begin to remake us.
As someone has put it: "Withdraw the emotional capital from the past and reinvest it in the future." To release a loved one is said to take an average of two years. It is a painful, hard period of time. Sometimes you cannot shorten it but must endure it in order to gain a new perspective.

"Job replied to the Lord: `I know that you can do all things; no plan of yours can be thwarted. You asked, "Who is this that obscures my counsel without knowledge?" Surely I spoke of things I did not understand, things too wonderful for me to know.'" (Job 42).

"God, your ways are right, and I did not understand them." Now Job is a new man with a new future. There is a future for Job because God has a future for him. There is a future for you because God has a future for you. You need not be fixated on the past. You need not stay back there. If you have gone through grief and deprivation, God can help you to reassess it and release it and then move on. He uses His people, and we will be a community of people who will stand with you in your grief. We won't say foolish things but will show you that we love you and we care. We just want to be there with you. Maybe we will sit silently and be available to you.

That's what the church should be saying. Maybe we'll give you a strong hug or a firm handshake. You will have the assurance of our availability, our care, prayers and love. All of us will have days when we will need the people of God to be a healing community in our lives.

Discovering Great Secrets

REMEMBER . . .
In the midst of your storm, remember this - regardless of how high the waves, He will be there in the boat with you. You can reach out and discover that God will meet you in your grief, for He is committed to you. It may be a long period of time, but He will walk with you through the valley.
Job discovered that life can become new. It can begin again.

THINKING IT OVER . . .
This is a topic that really does get through to us all at some point. So, let me make three applications about grieving.

(1) Grieving is necessary.
It is, just as long as it is a God given expression and a healthy release.

(2) Grieving can be good.
It is, just as long as we refuse the temptation to hide from the future.

(3) Grieving can be healthy.
It is, just as long as it ultimately refocuses on the living.

A widow had been married to a musician. He had died over twenty years earlier, yet she kept his music studio just as it was when he died. Refusing to allow anyone to enter, she locked the piano, never allowing anyone, not even herself, to play. Each day, she would come and stand at the open doorway, where she would unlock the piano and open it. She would stand there and be haunted for hours every day, by the memories of his music.

A Jewish rabbi wrote this wise comment, "The melody that the loved one played upon the piano of your life will never be played quite that way again."

ADMIT . . .
There will always be that hole; the loss of that dream, that expectation, that loved one. There will always be that gap. No

131

one will ever be able to play music like that one could. The rabbi went on to write: *"But we must not close the keyboard and allow the instrument to gather dust. We must seek out other artists of the spirit . . . who will walk the road with us."*

It's not what you and I have lost, but what we have left that counts now. This should become our focus. It is that which captivates our focus that ultimately, recreates joy. However, do not forget the process – *it takes time to heal.*

Discovering Great Secrets

FINALLY!

Great Delight In Me

Years ago I came across this passage in Zephaniah 3:17, "The LORD your God is with you, he is mighty to save. He will take great delight in you, he will quiet you with his love, he will rejoice over you with singing." I thought of my life.

I thought of what the passage says about God and how He feels about me.
He is mighty to save.
He will take great delight in me.
He will quiet me with His love.
He will rejoice over me.
I confessed that although I do not know if I fully understand what it means to be quieted by His love, I do know that there is something inside me that says, "I need that."

As I pondered more I prayed, Lord, please quiet me with Your love.
Lord, please quiet me with Your love.
Lord, please quiet me with Your love.
Lord, I get loud sometimes. Not so much verbally loud, but my spirit gets loud. My heart gets loud. My mind gets loud. The world around me gets loud and the loudness overwhelms me to the point that everything within me and around me seems to be loud.

So, Lord, please quiet me with Your love.
In these times of unrest and confusion in our nation and world I need to be quieted by Your love.

Decisions are being made that may well change the way we live and function as a people. Lord, please quiet me with Your love. As the years pass more rapidly than my mind can comprehend, I need to be quieted with Your love. I cannot keep up. I try, but I seem to fall farther and farther behind. Lord, please quiet me

Discovering Great Secrets

with Your love. In times of discouragement when I have failed to live as You have asked me to live I need to be quieted by Your love. In times of disappointment over dreams that have faded and when other people have failed to live up to my expectations, I need to be quieted by Your love.

Lord, please quiet me with Your love. In times of loss and when my heart has been broken, I need to be quieted by Your love. In times of sadness when a joyful spirit seems too much to consider, I need to be quieted by Your love. Lord, please quiet me with Your love. In times of suffering and pain as the result of another's actions or my own, I need to be quieted by Your love. In times of distress and anxiety over all that I must do, or feel that I must do, I need to be quieted by Your love. In times when life is so loud that I cannot hear my own thoughts, I need to be quieted by Your love. Lord, please quiet me with Your love. Unless You quiet me with Your love my life will surely be filled with noises that may drown Your voice from my ears.

Lord, I need to be quieted by Your love.
When I remind myself that You are with me.
When I contemplate Your power.
When I consider that You take great delight in me.
When I think of You rejoicing over me with singing because of Your love for me –
I am quieted. My heart is quieted.

My spirit rests.
"The LORD your God is with you, he is mighty to save. He will take great delight in you, he will quiet you with his love, he will rejoice over you with singing."

Discovering Great Secrets

NOTES
Some chapters are adapted from earlier books by Derek Stringer and now out of print.

Chapter 1
Books by Major W. Ian Thomas –
The Indwelling Life of Christ
The Saving Life of Christ
The Mystery of Godliness
Robert Boyd Munger –
My Heart, Christ's Home (Pamphlet, 1986)
David Dykes –
Discover Life Ministries (Transcripts) Internet: gabc.org
Chapter 2
G Campbell Morgan –
A Man Of The Word (Jill Morgan, 2010)
Ernest Shackleton –
Endurance: Shackleton's Incredible Voyage To The Antartic (Alfred Lansing, 2004)
Chapter 3
Murray McCheyne –
More Precious Than Gold (Mass Market, 2007)
Matthew Henry –
Commentary On The Whole Bible (Nelson, 2008)
Richard Baxter –
The Reformer Pastor (1974)
Murray Watts –
Hot Under The Collar (Monarch Publications)
John Stott –
The Gospel, The Spirit, The Church (STL, 1978)
Ray Stedman –
Discovery Papers – Authentic Christianity (1978)
Tony Campolo –
Who Switched The Price Tags (Word Books, 1986)
Chapter 4
James Dobson –
Quotes from Focus On the Family DVD
Corrie Ten Boom –
Prayer Powerpoints (Victor Books, p.109)

Discovering Great Secrets

C. S. Lewis –
Screwtape Letters (Fontana)
Thomas Chalmers –
Memoirs Of The Life And Writings Of Thomas Chalmers (Harper 2010)
Chapter 5
Philip Yancey –
Disappointed With God (Mass Market, 2003)
David Pawson –
Unlocking The Bible (With Andy Peck, 1999)
Tim Hansell –
You Gotta Keep Dancing: In The Midst Of Life's Hurts, You Can Choose Joy (1998)
Holy Sweat (1987)
Chapter 6
Stephen Brown –
A Scandalous Freedom (2004)
Mike Anders –
First Evangelical Free Church, Wichita (Transcripts)
Ray Pritchard –
Keep Believing Ministries (Transcript)
Chapter 7
Mike Anders –
First Evangelical Free Church, Wichita (Transcripts)
John Piper –
Desiring God Ministries (Transcript)
Charles Swindoll –
Walk With Jesus (Kindle, 2008)
Chapter 8
Philip Yancey –
Disappointed With God (Mass Market, 2003)
Bishop Ken Ulmer –
Sermon Quote (Faithful Central Bible Church, CA USA)
Chapter 9
Robert Browning –
Poet (Notable Works – The Pied Piper Of Hamelin. My Last Duchess)
Chapter 10
Jabez Bunting –

Discovering Great Secrets

English Wesleyan (Methodism And Social Change In Britain, J. Kent, 1977)
Calvin Miller –
Into The Depths Of God (Bethany House, 2001)
Peter Marshall –
A Man Called Peter (Catherine Marshall, Baker Publications, 1951)

Chapter 11
Stephen Brown –
When Being Good Isn't Good Enough (Crossway Books, 1991)
Arthur Custance –
Doorway Paper No.37 (Self Published)
Augustine –
Confessions (No.11)
Dennis Bennett –
Nine O'Clock In The Morning (Kingsway)

Chapter 12
John Claypool –
Tracks of a Fellow Struggler
C. S. Lewis –
A Grief Observed

Discovering Great Secrets